To Julie

With Luv & Best Wishes
xxx

Michael
Philip
Benton

6 Nov 2007

Mad Dogs and an Englishman

by
Michael Benton

AuthorHouse™ UK Ltd.
500 Avebury Boulevard
Central Milton Keynes, MK9 2BE
www.authorhouse.co.uk
Phone: 08001974150

This book is a work of non-fiction. Unless otherwise noted, the author and the publisher make no explicit guarantees as to the accuracy of the information contained in this book and in some cases, names of people and places have been altered to protect their privacy.

© 2007 Michael Benton. All rights reserved.

No part of this book may be reproduced, stored in a retrieval system, or transmitted by any means without the written permission of the author.

First published by AuthorHouse 10/4/2007

ISBN: 978-1-4343-3072-7 (sc)
ISBN: 978-1-4343-3071-0 (hc)

Printed in the United States of America
Bloomington, Indiana

This book is printed on acid-free paper.

Cover design and inserts by the Author
Front Cover: Author stranded in Iraqi desert
Back Cover: Garden Tomb in Jeruselum

This book is dedicated to my late mother **Mayvis Benton** without whose support it would never have been written

Contents

Introduction

Chapter One	Hello Europe	1
Chapter Two	Land of Myths and Legends	17
Chapter Three	Gateway to Asia	33
Chapter Four	The Road to the Holy Land	45
Chapter Five	The Garden Tomb	51
Chapter Six	Christmas in Jerusalem	57
Chapter Seven	The Rose Red City	65
Chapter Eight	Deep in the Desert	73
Chapter Nine	Iraq and Iran	83
Chapter Ten	A Maiden in Distress	89

Postscript

1. Stafford
2. Paris
3. Marseilles
4. Genoa
5. Naples
6. Brindisi
7. Igoumenitsa
8. Athens
9. Salonica
10. Athos
11. Istanbul
12. Ankara
13. Damascus
14. Beirut
15. Amman
16. Jerusalem
17. Petra
18. Akaba
19. Desert
20. Baghdad
21. Tehran
22. Isfahan
23. Kuwait

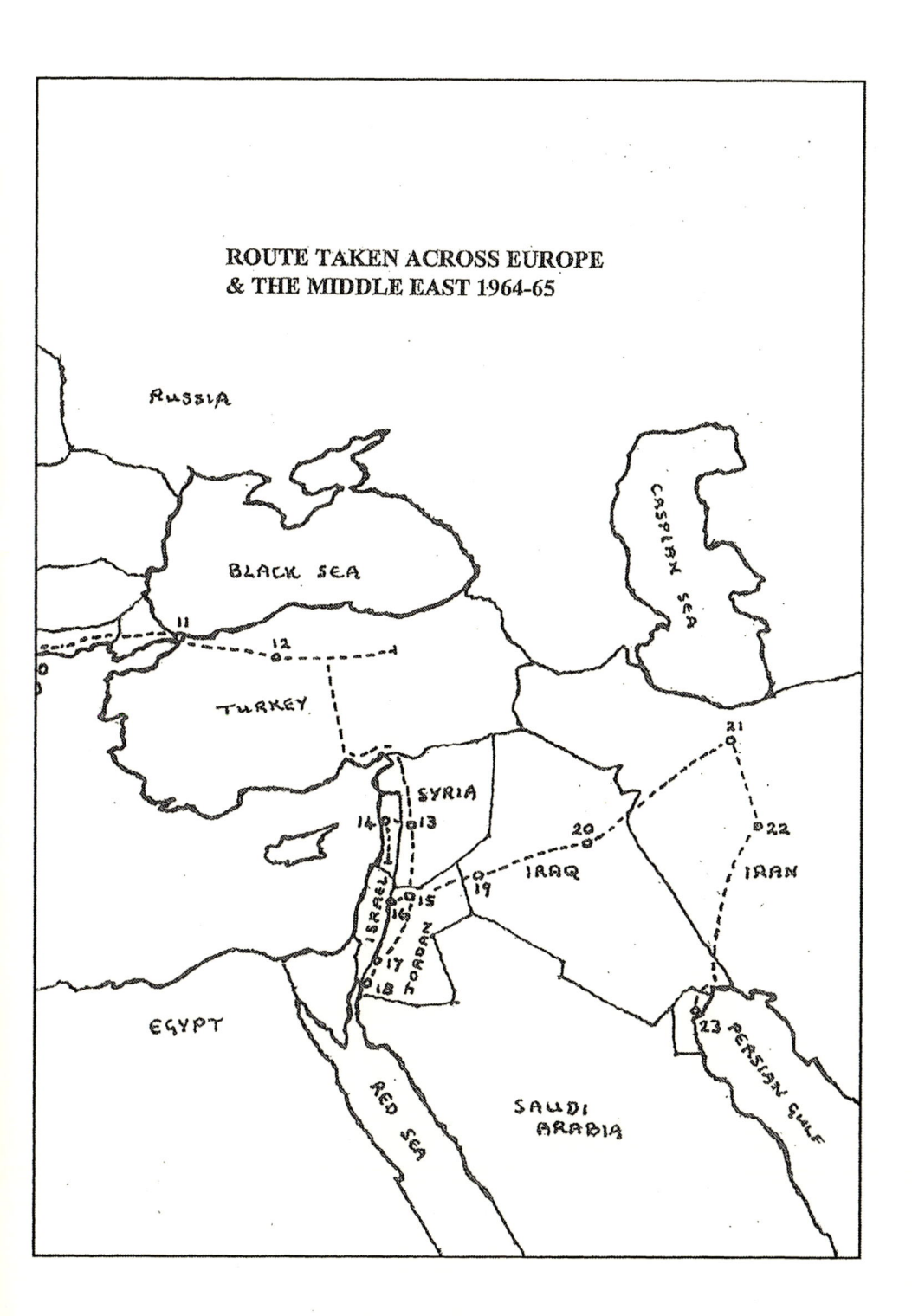

ROUTE TAKEN ACROSS EUROPE & THE MIDDLE EAST 1964-65

Introduction

This book was written forty years after the actual happenings, which may lead one to think that the memories would be fudged and faded with the passage of time. However, I can assure the reader this is not so for one very good reason. At the time of the travels I kept a diary and I also wrote letters regularly back home to my parents in England. My mother carefully kept every dated despatch, which she tied up neatly in a bundle and I discovered these when clearing her home thirty five years later. Reading the letters again brought back vivid memories of people and places, some of which I had partially or completely forgotten. Others of course were indelibly etched on my memory and will never fade. This led me to think perhaps I should record these experiences in a narrative to make easy reading for family and friends, some of whom I know are curious of my youthful escapades.

In 1964 this expedition was a dangerous adventure with a high degree of risk that perhaps only a young person with health and vigour could undertake. Today in 2007 it would be impossible to travel in some of these countries and survive. Forty years ago one could see the seeds developing of today's troubles in what is currently one of the worlds most horrific war zones. The experiences I gained of the character and culture of these peoples has had a big impact throughout the course of my life.

The western world is only just realising what a sensitive powder keg the Middle East has become. Our continued existence is really dependant on finding a solution to the Palestinian problem and how we all react and handle the resurgence of radical Islam.

Chapter One

Hello Europe

I was a young man of twenty-two years with a neat trimmed beard of jet-black hair, standing in new jeans, jumper and desert boots, which were donated by a Stafford shoe firm. My few belongings were packed into a framed rucksack given to me as a farewell present from colleagues at Staffordshire County Council. They had all signed their names under the flap with messages of good luck and hopes that I would eventually return safely to them.

Standing on the dockside at Dover I handed my pristine passport (attached by four feet of string to my belt) to the Customs Officer, who was a smart middle aged man in an immaculate uniform. He looked bemused at my attached passport then straight into my eyes.

'First time abroad Mr Benton?'

'Yes, I am off to see the world' I replied.

'Well may I wish you all the very best sir`

He smiled and waved me through, his words rang repeatedly in my ears as I walked up the ferry ramp, and nobody had ever called me 'sir` before yet there was a charm and sincerity in his manner. He had authority and concern, the likes of which I have never encountered at a passport control since and do not expect to ever again.

Strolling onto the top deck I went to the stern and lent on the rails. It was a warm August day and the cliffs of Dover shrank, as the channel waters grew wider. I pondered on where I was going and when I would see England again. Leaving a loving family and a good job to go where? It was not the thing then to go off travelling. The gap year had not been invented, the only people 'on the road' were tramps, miss-fits and a small number of young Australians trail blazing to and from the motherland. I was to meet a good number of them over the next year; they were generally hardened travellers with a network of contacts and essential advice for a novice like me.

On leaving home I had promised my tearful mother I would write regularly. I do not think she expected to ever see me again and my silent father did not know what to think. However, my letters were fairly regular and kept them advised of my well being. They also wrote regularly to me via 'Poste Restante' to the next city I was heading for. I still have most of those letters and they trigger memories of those hectic and exciting times.

Stepping off the ferry at Boulogne I passed through the port with no trouble and walked and walked in the direction of Paris. I thought I would hitch hike down through the middle of France to the warm Mediterranean. After a couple of hours I was picked up by an English couple who had spotted the handkerchief sized Union Flag on my rucksack. At least it had got me one lift and a sit down to rest my legs for a couple of hours. They were amused by my adventure and dropped me on the outskirts of Paris. It was getting dark and I needed to find a bed for the night. Coming across a park I wandered through and pitched my one pole, one rope tent within some shrubs. Taking off my walking boots I crawled into my new soft down sleeping bag. Very cosy and warm I was soon asleep. Waking to bird song the next morning my first night on foreign soil had passed in a flash. Keen to move on I rolled up my sleeping bag and packed it, with my tent, back into my rucksack and left the park.

Somehow I needed to cross or circumnavigate Paris to get onto the south side and find the N5 south. The roads were getting busy and buildings bigger. The pavements were hard, my legs tired and I thought I would be walking forever. Feeling the need for breakfast I found a bread shop, a French stick and a cake. Such lovely cakes, I had never seen such a variety; I could have eaten half a dozen but for the price. Sitting on a street bench I consumed half the loaf, the cake and half a bottle of water while contemplating the strategy for putting Paris behind me. Most people would have wanted to go in and see the sights but I was not so keen, it would be too hectic and too expensive. I had left England with five pounds in cash and ten Travellers Cheques of five pounds secreted in a money belt around my waist. This money has to last me a long time and I am finding France much more expensive than England. Ten shillings (50p) for a light meal, half a crown (12½ p) for a coffee! But a glass of beer or wine was only six pence (2½ p).

I could get drunk before I could quench my thirst, oh well! I walk on; Paris is big, much bigger than I had thought. It is like London, so I will get a bus. Nobody seems to speak English, well not to me anyway. I climb on a bus and sit down getting some loose change out of my pocket. The conductor asks me something, so I say Paris and give him some money. He looks puzzled and walks away talking to himself. I sit and watch the buildings getting bigger and grander. The conductor keeps looking at me and walking up and down. After about ten minutes he comes up to me and points to the door. Now, I have either had my monies worth or he does not want me on the bus any more. We are in busy streets now and I guess I must be fairly central. I need to find someone who can speak English and give me some directions. Paris is so much bigger than I expected and seems to stretch forever. I walk and walk through the bustling streets. The French are terrible drivers; they do not have as many cars on the road, yet they seem to be continually bumping into each other. I have counted eight crashes since entering Paris. Walking on and on I believe I am moving southwards but soon it will be dark and I need to find another park to settle down for the night. The next morning I wake early, pack my bag, find breakfast in a back street café and move on to find the main road south. After finding a suitable hitching point and waiting for hours, I am eventually picked up by a French man and his teenage son. They are very amiable and chatty even though they don't speak any English and my French is next to nil. I have not yet met anyone who can speak English or admit to it. I find it strange that when I ask in one shop for the Petite Pain (a roll of bread) I am offered it straight away whereas in another shop the assistant shrugs their shoulders and walks away.

The French man and his son seem genuinely keen to converse with me and we travel through Fontainebleau and stop for a break in

Auxerre where we walk around the town and visit the Cathedral, a large medieval stone building, heavily carved with vast numbers of statues. There happens to be a service in progress, but here the congregation wander in and out and walk around as if they are in a market place. The choir and clergy seem to be the only ones participating in the service. My new companions go inside and I follow, they sit down for five minutes then stand up and walk around looking at the sculpture just like sightseers. Then we go out and return to the car. We had been to church! Travelling on south we part company at Tournes and I continue my way onto Marseille.

Having got a lift into the centre of Marseille I wander the streets and I'm shocked at the large number of down and outs lying on the pavements. I am told there are many immigrants following an uprising in Algiers resulting in much poverty and unemployment. The air here is so still, stuffy and hot that yesterday I drank four bottles of wine costing me four shillings (20p). Sitting exhausted in a café I am approached by two students who speak a little English. They take me to a bus stop and explain where there is a campsite I could use. They give me a bus ticket, which you should buy from a tobacconist. Now that probably explains why I was evicted from the bus in Paris. This time I am permitted to sit the journey out being advised where to get off and the conductor pointing out the camping site. It is only a short walk to the house where, on seeing my union flag, the lady offers me a chair and hurries away. After a few minutes she returns with a man who approaches me saying 'Are you English'?

'Yes' I reply 'I am looking for a pitch for my tent'.

'Good, I am Athol from Yorkshire, we will fill in the entrée card and then you can come with me'.

He takes me along to his caravan at the back of the site, suggesting I take a shower while he prepares a meal. While we eat Athol tells me he is happy for me to stay in his caravan, he would enjoy speaking English for a change and so would I for that matter. He is the first person I have met who can speak English since I left England. Athol continues to tell of his adventures, by trade he is a painter and decorator and left England when he was in his thirties for a painting contract in Holland. He has worked in various European countries slowly building up his business, then he won a contract to decorate King Feisal's palace in

Arabia he was doing very well with 200 workmen and everything he needed, then the revolution came and he was very lucky to escape in his big American car with a few personal possessions.

He has been hiding out on the campsite for over a year, as he likes Marseille and the climate. He works illegally decorating for seven pounds a week, he pays one shilling a night for his caravan so he gets by nicely as his only other expenses are food and petrol. The Gendarmes have a search for him every now and again but they have only caught him once and then it cost him twenty pounds. His big American car still carries Arabic plates and he leaves for work early in the morning to miss the traffic, then he speeds through the town so fast nothing can catch him. His tales go on and on. It is such a relief to relax in comfort and feel secure, Athol agrees to me staying with him for a few days and while he is at work I can work at assembling lavatory brushes for my keep. This is a sideline he has acquired for a bit of cash, it is very easy to do but extremely boring.

When I tell him one evening that I think I should be moving on or perhaps getting a job locally he suggests grape picking at a vineyard he knows. He writes me a letter of introduction to a Madam Malet at Chateauneuf in the province of Var. The next morning he takes me at 5am on his way to work, dropping me on the road to Var to hitch a lift. For most of the journey I travel in a Citroen 2CV with a French farmer who says nothing. I have never been in a 2CV before and it is a little disconcerting watching the road speed by beneath my feet through the gaps in the floor. I decide to keep very still and not look down and before too long he is dropping me at the gates of Chateauneuf. After a long walk up the drive and through the gatehouse I wander around this huge ancient and picturesque castle like mansion. I find a man who shows me through the back door and takes me to Madam Malet. A tiny lady dressed totally in black, she has a huge bunch of keys hanging from her belt. She looks hard at me as I give her Athol's letter, then she grunts, says, "Yes" and rattles away in French to the man who had shown me in. The introduction appeared to work well. I was taken to the gatehouse and shown a very nice sitting room with bedroom and bathroom alongside. I am told 'Today you are free, tomorrow you work'.

I spend the evening exploring the grounds and garden of this huge house with its towers and courtyards sitting in the rolling hills, which are covered in row after row of vines. I did not realise at that time this is in fact the famous Chateauneuf Vineyard. Tomorrow I will be out there somewhere picking grapes, [little did I know what I was in for]. After a good nights sleep I wash in a civilised manner and make my way to the rear of the house meeting up with other workers. We all congregate in a large hall, which appears to be a scullery off the main kitchen. No ovens or chefs here, but tables of raw food yet to be prepared. Baskets of bread and five gallon tins of French jam. The other workers are breaking open the rolls of fresh bread and spreading it with butter and jam from the tins. There are also slices of dark, dry ham and oranges and grapes galore. This is breakfast with coffee of course and I join in until I am full. After half an hour or so there is a shout from the French gang master and I follow the group outside. There are about a dozen of us walking alongside the tractor, which is towing a trailer stacked with empty baskets. Some are like log baskets with two handles, others are black or green, heavy duty plastic ones. The tractor leads the way and some of the pickers sit on the trailer to save their legs. When we reach the picking zone each picker is given a basket, a pair of secateurs and allocated a vine line. These vines are about two feet high and three wide. The grapes grow in large bunches with black berries as big as conkers with a morning mist and cobwebs spread over them. They taste sweet and juicy and there are lots of them, acres and acres. After an hour my hands are sticky and covered with grape juice. It is taking me twice as long to fill a basket as the other pickers. Most of them I discover are Spanish, who come each year for the harvest and they work fast and long. When your basket is full you carry it to the trailer and tip it in. The French overseer keeps a check on his worksheet of each worker's basket count. This must mean you are paid by the basket and I do not think he noticed me put my last basket in the trailer. So I must make a point of walking past him or catch his eye each time I tip. The sun is starting to get warm and the back of my head is getting hot. Fortunately I have brought my water bottle with me and it should last me until lunchtime, which cannot come soon enough.

At noon we all return to the house for lunch. Plate after plate of the most amazing concoctions, things I have never seen before. I cannot eat half of what they put on my plate and there is growing concern that I am not eating enough. Madam Malet is called for and after discussion she instructs that I can choose which food I want to eat. So now they give me anything I ask for and I eat my fill of the choicest food at every mealtime, though I still have difficulty in eating all of my allocated melon each day. Later I realise that this amazing kitchen also supplies the exclusive restaurant at the front of the chateau, which serves some of the finest cuisine in France. Madam Malet is a tiny, willow the wisp like figure who appears to be everywhere, issuing orders and ruling her little empire very strictly and efficiently. I discover there is also a Monsieur Malet but he is very old and infirm. He spends most of his time sitting in the courtyard under a straw hat with a glass of wine in his hand. He plays no part whatsoever in the management of the Chateau, maybe he did once but now it is all controlled by the very efficient Madam.

Lunchtime is long and lazy, I feel the heat of the sun and too soon we are back on the hillside. In half an hour my red stained sticky hands are blistering with friction against the handles of the secateurs. I try using them in my left hand but that is awkward and much slower. I am already way behind in the basket count so I will have to put up with the blisters. This afternoon the vines are becoming smaller and the bunches fewer. Other delays and hazards occur such as brambles that scratch and hungry wasps that sting. Then I get a bite from what looks like a praying mantis about nine inches long.

By the end of the afternoon my back is very uncomfortable, the sun burning, my throat parched and my hands scratched, blistered and covered in sticky juice and blood. Grape picking sounded so idyllic but the reality is very different. It is very hard work and the French avoid it, that's why they need to bring in the Spaniards who I never thought of as being particularly hard working. However, they can all out pick me. The seven p.m. knock off never comes early enough, then we can all saunter back to the house, I wash my hands and eat whatever I can find in the outer kitchen and then retire early to bed. The other pickers wait until about eight thirty pm for a larger meal when they all sit down eating and drinking well into the night. My rooms are quiet and well away from the buzz of the chateau. After a couple of days a black sheep dog called Romulus adopts me; he follows me everywhere, even sleeping at the base of my bed. I am woken one night by running water and on searching for the source I find it is Romulus, who has learnt how to turn the tap on the bidet in order to get a drink. He is constantly at my side except in the heat of the day when he wisely retires to the shade beneath the trailer.

Life in the chateau is an education. There are grand rooms at the front where the workers are not allowed but from time to time you could catch a glance of the splendour through an open door. Then in the middle of the house there is the office and workrooms. [I only ever went to the office twice, the day I arrived and the day I left]. The day I arrived I gave my details and handed my passport to Madam Malet who opened a wall safe with a key from the big bunch on her belt. When she opened the safe I was amazed to see bricks of French notes tied up neatly with string. She placed my passport inside and locked the safe. Did she think I was going to run away?

The rear of the chateau is rambling and beside the large kitchen where only the cooks are allowed there is a huge outer kitchen come scullery where all the workers mingle. They sit about, eat and await their orders. Madam Malet is in and out regularly to check on who was doing what. It is where deliveries come in and food and goods are checked before going to their respective storerooms. It is like going back two hundred years in time. This must have been how the old manor houses of England used to be run and obviously some still are in France. I am not too impressed with the French to date. They appear ignorant, aloof and not very clean in their habits. They grunt, cough and splutter, even spit on the stone floors in the house. Mind you they do go outside to relieve themselves though they're not fussy where or who may be passing at the time. The Spanish are cleaner, courteous and definitely subservient in this establishment.

There is a constant babble of French and Spanish that at times sounds like a language race, which on occasions erupts into a shouting match with bread rolls being hurled from one person to another. When things start flying Romulus and I go out and sit in the courtyard. Day after day passes by in such monotonous drudgery, picking grapes all day and sleeping all night, interspersed with wholesome meals, coffee and red wine. If it was not for the backbreaking grape picking I could endure this life style. After some four weeks I think the picking must come to an end soon before my back breaks, but no they keep finding more hills and more vines to pick. I make up my mind that by the end of the week I will go. I go to tell Madam, she looks alarmed 'Oh non' she tried everything to keep me but she had few words of English 'we talk tomorrow'. I am also concerned that I may be working for very little because she would never talk money. I have even written to Athol for his advice and he wrote back saying do not worry she will not pay you until you finish but she will see you alright in the end.

The next morning Madam comes to me with a lady who speaks English. I explain that I have to move on, as my time is up. Madam it appears wants me to stay several more weeks until the end of the season. I am assured my work is appreciated and there is much work yet to do and the rains may come before all the harvest is in. No, I insist I must go (because my back is killing me). Carrying my rucksack will be easy after this. Finally, Madam says, "Okay" and beckons me to follow her to collect my passport and hopefully some money. Her jangling keys find the keyhole in the safe and she reaches in for my passport and hands it to me. Then she turns again to the safe and takes a small wedge of money, she does not count it she just passes it to me saying 'merci beaucoup'. I have no idea how much she has paid me for my five weeks hard labour. She mumbles about the grapes, the wine and something about Romulus. Parting from Romulus has not been upper most in my mind. When I go to collect my things and pack my bag he knows I am going. He looks very sad as sheep dogs can and follows closely watching my every move. I try to say goodbye when I close the door but he follows me down the drive. Oh dear, is he going to keep following me. He is such a good-natured and obedient dog but now it is painful for both of us. Fortunately arrangements have been made for me to have a lift in a van to Nice, so I am able to prevent him getting in the van with me. He stands on the roadside and watches me disappear.

I often wondered how long he waited for me to return. He must have eventually returned home for his dinner as some time later when I wrote to thank Madam Malet she did write back a short note saying Romulus was missing me.

Free from bondage I count my money and it works out at a pound a day. That's hard work for the money, particularly as I am not used to hard labour. The backache is a reminder I will carry for some time. My previous experience of physical work has been vocational jobs during the summer when I was at Stafford Art College. One year a few of us students went sketching at Chipperfields Circus, which was on summer tour in Cannock. They were recruiting for tent boys and animal grooms. My friend Duggie and I got taken on as elephant grooms for five pounds per week. That was another story but the lasting memory of that job was the smell that hung on us for days after we left. Another summer the college crew signed up for lumber jacking on Cannock Chase for six pence a tree, the lasting memory of that was blistered hands and dust. Going home at the end of the day as dirty as any coal miner. I mused over which job I could have taken on for the longest period of time, I could not decide.

After some four hours drive I am dropped in the centre of Nice. It is eleven p.m. and I am picked up by the police and taken to a camping site on the edge of town.

The following day I am given a lift to Monte Carlo by a French boy on holiday. His father is a diplomat and he likes to spend money. We go into the grand part of Monaco and have a fabulous lunch; he then goes shopping to buy gold-rimmed sunglasses and a tweed cap! We lounge around posing on the sea front; I think we must look an odd pair. He takes me further along the coast road towards Genoa and leaves me at a camping site before returning to France.

Forgetting I am now in Italy I struggle with my French and it is with great relief that I find some Italians who can speak English. The following day I make it to Genoa, which has a large port with ships from all over the world, so maybe I can find one to take me on. The port entrance is guarded with police and port guards. After some clumsy conversation and sign language, looking perplexed they allow me through. Walking the long quayside I search in vain for a friendly flag. Spotting a Dutch ship I climb the gangway and call to a couple of lads. They speak good English and welcome me aboard. While drinking tea they tell me they have just arrived from South Africa laden with fruit, some of which they try to load off onto me but I could not carry more than a few apples and oranges. They think they have seen a union flag at the far end of the quay but as it is a long walk and almost dark I wait until tomorrow.

Refreshed I make my way out of the port gate with another hard look from the police. Walking the coast road I come across a cable car, so I take that up the hill in search of a quiet spot. At the top is a small village with a water tap so I top up my bottle and look for a tent pitch. When I find a spot I light a fire and cook some spaghetti and rice and follow that with a ships apple. I then roll myself in the tent and bed down for the night. The wind gets stronger in the early hours and it is so strong I have to strap my rucksack to myself to secure it. The wind roars and it is a very disturbing night. By dawn the wind has dropped and I am dozing off when suddenly there is gunfire and bullets whistling over my head. Grabbing my jumper I wave it furiously above my head while I lay flat on the ground. When the shooting stops I slowly rise up peering across the hillside to see four men with rifles spaced out and approaching me. One calls out and the others are laughing and grinning. I do not know whether it was a comment to me or about me but they walk on pursuing rabbits I believe. After a light breakfast of bread and cheese, I head back down on the cable car to the port.

Returning to the barrier I have no difficulty in walking through and out along the quay. Passing ship after ship it seems they come from every country except England; from Russia, Japan, France, Israel, but nowhere can I see a Union Jack. Then at last, there it is, on just about the last ship in port. I climb the long ladder up her side. At the top is a middle aged man looking as rough as I do, he challenges me in a foreign tongue and it is obvious he does not understand me. While we try to communicate another man hearing the commotion comes over. He is English and invites me on board explaining as we walk that all the ships are allocated an Italian guard commonly known as a 'watch dog'. It appears that it is popular practice for men out of work to look for jobs on the ships in port. The authorities discourage this and allocate attendants to each ship to monitor the comings and goings. The watch dogs deter any but their own countrymen who, if successful in getting a job pass the watchdog a tip.

We soon arrive at the mess and tea is called for. We sit in a windowless room where the tables and benches are bolted to the floor. 'Chippy' the engineer, introduces me to three other lads, deckhands and donkey greasers, and they all give me a warm welcome. Chippy tells me I can stay on board while they are in port, which he expects to be for another four days. However, the decision on whether I could sail would be with the captain and he is indisposed with an alcoholic headache today and probably tomorrow as well. In the meantime Chippy says he can find me a job painting the ships railings with red oxide, I can eat with the crew and sleep in the lounge. He makes it sound so simple really. No money though, I will get my keep and if I am good they will take me ashore in the evenings. The food is more than adequate, not so tasty as Chateauneuf but mountains of it. The left overs from one meal alone are eight fish, three loaves of bread, pastries and a pile of potatoes and they all go over the side. "Feeding the fishes," I am told. Painting the railings is tedious, rail after rail, on and on. The red oxide is like painting with tar, it looks hideous and stains anything it touches, particularly my hands. The ship is called 'The Montcalm' and there is a brass plaque on her deck in the memory of a crewmember who lost his life in the rescue of the Laconia a few years earlier.

Come the evening Chippy and two of the hands say they are going ashore and invite me to join them. I do not know what to expect but they say it is their only entertainment. Most of them drink freely when in port and will think nothing of spending £50 on drink in a few days. It will probably be weeks before they would reach land again. One hand tells me he never goes ashore and in three months he has saved £500 whereas another lad spends whenever he can and only has five shillings in his pocket. The two of them had joined the ship at the same time but were like chalk and cheese.

In the evening we walk out through the gates, now the guards ignore me and I can come and go at will. The men know where they are going, to a place called 'Nick and Pat's' bar along what is known as the Barbary Coast. Inside it's done out similar to an English pub. There is the choice of a Jukebox for customers to select and pay, or an Italian radio for free. We sit around a table playing cards and drinking lager and whisky. The hostess is an Italian lady in her forties called Maria, she appears to know Chippy and the lads well and it is a very friendly atmosphere. She brings pastries from the kitchen and spends most of the evening sitting with us chatting and playing cards, it is rather like a family get together of yesteryear. In the early hours after they have drunk about eight pints and I have managed three we all stagger back to the Montcalm and into bed without incident.

On the third day I am painting the rails on deck when a middle-aged man in a leather jacket comes by and stops at my side. 'Who took you on?' he demanded. I guess this is the captain with a sore head.

' I am just helping out while you are in port'

'Hmm nobody told me' he retorts as he continues on his way muttering. Chippy tells me later that the captain would not allow me to sail. Sadly I bid farewell to the friendly crew the next morning and travel a few more miles along the coast road. At nightfall I roll up in the tent in a railway cutting and sleep heavily to wake the next morning rain-soaked. I find my breakfast and the cork from my wine bottle has been eaten, presumably by rats. Up and on the road two hours later I am in Pisa and then onto Florence, courtesy of an American. He tells me his son is about to travel Europe just like me and he wonders how much money he should give him for two months. Do I think that five hundred pounds would be enough? I tell him I had done it on less than fifty.

Today my umbrella fell to pieces, so I replace it with a straw sun hat. I arrive on the outskirts of Naples at 10pm and pitch my tent next to a couple of Australians on tour in a VW camper. They tell me they have done eighteen countries and have fifteen to go; they intend to spend winter in England and hope to get work there to replenish their finances. After breaking camp I make for the docks but find them very heavily guarded due to smuggling. I slip in by walking between two lines of lorries and the second ship I come to is British, the 'Hacienda'. On boarding I come across the mate who takes me to see the master. An extremely nice fellow, he takes me in, we eat, drink and chat for a couple of hours. He tells me he was the master of the Montcalm when the Laconia went down. Regulations will not allow him to take me to sea but I am welcome to join them onboard while in port and he could give me work painting the galley. The first mate and the boatswain take to me but the majority of the crew, being Italian, keep to themselves. One evening the mate takes me to see the Seaman's Mission, an ancient hall where there are shops, a chapel and a dance hall, available to all seafarers of all nationalities, but very English in its atmosphere. At that moment a storm blows up and I am called upon to assist with emergency moorings and the battening of hatches. A Dutch ship a few hundred yards along the quay suddenly goes down and the crew have to be taken off by helicopter. The dockers rush onto our deck to get a better view and are frantic with excitement.

On returning to the dock gate last night, I was refused entry but an English sailor lent me his pass and I gained access through another gate. The captain has now given me a pass but the gate guards also want cigarettes, which I do not have. The captain tells me he has to bribe the dockers with two hundred cigarettes each before they will unload his cargo. The current cargo is milk powder (a free gift from the USA). It took a day to load the ship in the States but in Naples it has taken three days so far and is still not half unloaded. Then there is the cigarette bond. At sea the crew can buy limitless cigarettes from the ships shop, a packet of twenty for a shilling [five pence]. In port however, the shop is closed and customs officers come on board every day to count the cigarettes. It costs the captain five hundred cigarettes a day before their totals tally. Life on ship in port is very good; I sample some of the finest wine and cigars in the world. The boatswain told me that on the Canadian trip he could stock up with Spanish wine and make a profit of five hundred pounds. So I left yet another British ship having been well fed and rested. I hit the road once again, this time for Pompeii. Here I meet two American servicemen on leave from Germany, we join forces for a tour of the ruins, which are quite impressive and thought provoking. After sightseeing, we go into town for a meal and return to my camp where we sing folk songs until we fall asleep. The next day the Americans head for Rome and I go south for Brindisi. On the road the local children follow me everywhere asking for sweets and cigarettes. I have to be careful they do not steal from my rucksack while I walk. They gather in small groups behind me and try to pilfer, so I have to keep turning around unexpectedly.

I am now well down the western side of the leg of Italy. I have to cross the Italian mountains from Salerno to Taranto some two days drive by car, but I am advised not to attempt the journey on foot, as I will never get a lift. However, I need to get to the Adriatic crossing point of Brindisi or spend many days going back up the 'leg' of Italy to return back down the eastern coast.

Pushing on I do get a lift to Potensa and spend the night with locals in little more than a shack. We are high up and the air is cold. The custom is to drink and dance and as a guest I am expected to dance with everyone in turn, men as well. They wear such large heavy boots that mine look like ballet shoes in comparison. The next day we move on, mile after mile of dirt track, no sign of another vehicle just mules and oxen. After two days I arrive in Brindisi hungry and weary. A small town its main feature is the wharf; this is the Italian ferry point to the east. I meet up with a group of travellers awaiting the next ferry for Greece. I am approached by a burly Scotsman by the name of Archie, who introduces me to a New Zealander known as 'Kiwi' who is travelling courtesy of a private income, which keeps him in drink and us amused by his antics. Then there is a large ex navy American, a gentle giant of a man travelling with an Australian girl. Then there is Dave from Newcastle, an ex paratrooper and a veteran of Cyprus who takes lead of our little band of explorers. Dave knows the Middle East well and speaks some of the lingo. He carries a sheath knife, which makes mine look like a nail file, plus a Beretta pistol, which he says he rarely has to use. The six of us catch the ferry that night for Igoumenitsa in Greece. The state of the boat and the weight of its cargo make me wonder if it will keep afloat long enough to reach Greece. My comment to Dave brings the response

"Why man its been floating back and forth for years".

A few years later back in England I heard a news bulletin that the floating wreck had ceased to float with considerable loss of life.

Chapter Two

Land of Myths and Legends

Greece appears not just like another country but another world as we draw along-side the quay at Igoumenitsa. It is raining heavily and there is little or nothing of a town just a small village. The main road leads off up into the hills. Kiwi walks off on his own, Dave and Archie are fortunate in finding a lift and the other travellers coming off the ferry disperse. This leaves Lee [an American I met on the ferry] and myself to make our way in the dark and the pouring rain. We come to a building that looks like it could be a village hall, where we try to seek shelter. Initially the door is opened by a non-English speaking man who takes one look at us two drowned rats and closes the door again. Continuing to hammer the door, it is eventually opened again, this time by a young English man who invites us in. It turns out to be a VSO unit (Voluntary Service Overseas) working on a water project for the locality, which is being manned by young people from England. We are invited to take off our wet clothes and have hot coffee with chats all round followed by a comfortable bed for the night.

In the morning we are out walking the road again or should I say track. Hoping for a lift to Ioannina and eventually onto Athens, we walk and walk for much of the time with the occasional short lift from village to village. The scenery is magnificent, towering rocky mountains with cliff faces rising up from bright green fields, fruit laden trees and repeated land slides spilling out across the road due to the torrential rain. Fantastic cloud formations swirl around us, with heavy showers, interspersed with bright sunshine that makes everything sparkle. It really is a land of mystery and magic and just like living in a Greek myth; it is easy to see what inspired their authors. Eventually we reach Agrinion, a small town with very few people. It looks like being another very wet night so we book into a hotel for four shillings (20p) to ensure a dry and comfortable night.

The next day we make good time, have a substantial lunch of fish salad, fruit and wine and continue travelling through beautiful countryside. I fell in love with Greece at first sight and still love it forty years later. The following day we reach Athens and book into a youth hostel near the centre. Hotels in Athens are much more expensive and so we are obliged to down grade to a hostel. However, it is clean, comfortable and better than many hotels that we have stayed in previously. Today is Sunday and entry to museums and historic sights are free, so after washing our clothes and changing some money we make for the Acropolis. On the way we come across a street market, selling every conceivable type of old junk imaginable, including crashed cars and broken pots, pans and crockery; things you would only expect to find down the tip in England but lined up on the roadside here being peddled for pennies. Now its time for lunch with a Greek concoction of sardines, feta cheese, melon and Turkish delight, washed down with the local Ouzo, a strong anis-based liquor. Replenished we set off on the long trek up the hill to the Parthenon. It looks just like in the films, only bigger. The blocks of stone are massive and the space is huge. You walk and walk and seem to cover no ground. The views are spectacular and I was overcome with the timeless wonderment. For countless years people had come here and marvelled; for centuries before people had worked, pleasured and worshipped on this huge manmade stone hill planning banquets and sacrifices to conquer the world.

I am getting on well with my American companion; he is strong and tough, an ex-marine who has seen action in Vietnam. He is a good guy to have around and while in Athens we visit the American base where he gets a cholera shot and collects some chlorination tablets. On the way back we pass a hotel where there is a party going on. We cautiously look inside to find it full of young English-speaking folk. Some are making for a Kibbutz in Israel, others for India and some for London. A Greek boy explains that today is the feast of Saint Demetrius and we should pay our respects to the old man upstairs. We both climb to the top of the house and are presented with a piece of cake by an old lady in black. She takes us through to see an old man said to be in his nineties, sitting in a mini art gallery. He used to be a professor of art at the Athens Academy and enjoys showing his quite impressive and numerous canvasses. After viewing we are ushered out and handed a chocolate as a parting gift.

Before we travel on I feel I ought to replace the little union flag on my rucksack. The original one is now tatty, frayed at the bottom and has lost its colour to the sun. It looks like an old handkerchief flapping from the top of my rucksack. Why bother flying the flag you may ask. Well when you are hitch- hiking people would like to know where you are from before they stop. From your national flag they can deduce your language and culture. They will know whether they will be able to communicate with ease or not at all and the union flag indicates the English language. Cultural identity is also important; for example, it was extremely difficult getting a lift in France when flying the flag and almost as difficult in Germany. I even had one motorist slow down and shout from his car 'go home Jew boy'. I never managed to work out why he thought I was Jewish. In Greece I found the opposite reaction. Nearly everyone wants to stop and talk with you, even if they can only say 'hello' and are only going to the next village. When they stop you are obliged to get in, smile, nod and often end up half an hour later, being introduced to their family and neighbours. If it is late in the day an evening meal and a bed for the night may be inevitable. Such is the hospitality of the Greeks, or it was in the 1960's. Maybe they are not so enthusiastic these days with the huge growth in tourism? The Greeks I have always found to be a warm, generous and friendly people. They tend to appreciate knowledge even when they cannot write, art when they cannot draw and music when they cannot sing. They are well aware of their cultural past and are proud of it. Yet never have I seen that drive to conquer the world that you can encounter in some of the countries that I was yet to reach. On that first visit I felt so at home with the people, the climate and the food, I felt I had always lived there. It fitted me like a well-worn suit. No other country has ever given me that same feeling; hence I have had the pleasure of returning many times since. I remember finding it difficult to understand why I should feel this way so far from home when in France, only twenty miles from England, I felt in an alien world.

So I move on to find a replacement flag, which I purchase in a souvenir shop near the city centre. The shop owner, Frixtos begins to take special interest when I pin the new flag on my rucksack, and he wants to know where we are going next. Within minutes he has adopted us and wants to show us his new campsite at Refina. We must come back later when he closes his shop, so we can stay with him and his friends for the weekend at his new campsite. On returning we find Frixtos and three of his friends waiting for us with a hamper full of food. We all squeeze into his car and he drives us out of the City and along the coast road for about an hour, then he turns off and drives through fields, then sand dunes and finally onto the beach. I do not know what to expect, but I am surprised to find no hint of any development. A rather deserted yet picturesque beach and shoreline stretching as far as the eye can see. There was a stony stretch and three very basic chalets with a small brick built toilet and shower. Is this the campsite? Not quite, there are also two rather large flagpoles that have escaped my attention until Frix unfolds two large flags that he has brought along from the shop; a Greek flag and a Union flag, which he immediately hoists up the poles before even unpacking the car or opening the chalet. Lee is a bit miffed and asks me quietly,

"Where's the Stars and Stripes?"

"Well there are only two poles," I reply,

"Those poles are big enough to fly three flags from each pole," he retorts.

Then I realise Frix thinks that we are both English.

"Can't he tell I have an American accent?" asks Lee.

"Obviously not, he just recognises that you speak English." I reply.

We all muck in to set up the barbeque and bring out stools and a table from the chalet. There are some good-sized fish, some potatoes, paprika and tomatoes already prepared on skewers. While the barbeque gets going we all chat and there is a babble of Greek, English and Anglo-American Greek. Soon we are all tucking into fish and chips Greek-style, washed down with local red wine and Retsina. Now Retsina I believe is an acquired taste and one I have never persevered to attain. I am told it is brewed from the sap of pine trees and from the taste of it, probably trees frequented by dogs. It is amber in colour and could easily be mistaken for old-fashioned antiseptic cleaning fluid. My recommendation is not to travel more than six inches to experience it. We also have flat bread like thick pancakes, which we heat on the grill. Each round Frix takes from the grill, he makes the sign of a cross on it with his finger, mutters a few words, tears it in half and hands it round. I remember thinking I hope this isn't our last supper.

When we have eaten our fill we drink coffee and talk; Frix speaks at length about his plans to develop the camping site. He thinks he has enough ground to build about twenty chalets and pitches for about a hundred tents. As there is no fence or boundary it is impossible to calculate the size of his territory. Frix asks us to please return to England and tell everybody about his wonderful campsite. Next year he is certain it will be bustling with bathers and barbeques. We talk well on into the night until all the wine has been consumed, finally going to bed at about two thirty in the morning. The next morning we rise late, have a light breakfast and then go for a swim in the Aegean Sea. The water is not as warm as I like it so I come out and dry off while the others continue to swim. Then idle the day away before returning to Athens in the late afternoon.

That evening back at our little hotel 'Madam Lilly's' at 18 Marseille Street we meet a man who is going to Salonika the next day. Lee chats him up for a lift, which he agrees to. It is a good stretch that could take a week using local transport and he is expecting to do it in a day. We travel well on the best road we have yet seen in Greece. However, some twenty miles short of our destination we come across a road accident. In the Greek tradition the driver stops to help and we end up taking one of the injured women to hospital. It is one o'clock in the morning before we leave the hospital and he drops us off at a little café in the city centre. We have bread and soup and rest there until daybreak. The next day we look around Salonika, which is rather boring after Athens so we decide to move on east and catch a lift in a car to Arnaia, a village in the middle of nowhere. It is getting dark so we walk on looking for a place to pitch the tent. We are very tired having not had a bed the night

Michael Benton

before, so as it is dry we think we can get by without actually putting up the tent. We find what looks like an abandoned roofless house so we use the tent as a ground sheet and snuggle into our sleeping bags.

We awake abruptly the next morning to the rising sun in our eyes and a flock of some fifty bleating sheep literally on top of us. Startled, we struggle to our feet to find two shepherds leaning over the wall above us, laughing their heads off. We have unknowingly spent the night in a sheep pen. We make our way between the frightened sheep and around to the back wall where the shepherds are still laughing. They are friendly, inquisitive and wishing to inspect our sleeping bags. They are wearing the strangest coats I have ever seen. A very stiff woven fabric in wool and straw, T-shaped and full length. They let us try them on and I found them very heavy and uncomfortable, a bit like trying to wear a carpet, but obviously warm and weather proof. After gating the sheep in the pen they invite us back to their house in the village where we all sit down to melon, pomegranate and Ouzo. We cannot converse with them, but by now Lee and I are experts at nodding and grinning. We have made their day and they enjoy showing their women what they have found in their sheep pen. The ladies do not think it so humorous but keep smiling and plying us with fruit and Ouzo to keep the men happy. By now Lee and I are becoming accustomed to the Greek hospitality and not too surprised when one man slips away only to return minutes later with his neighbour, wife and their children. We guess that in no time at all the whole village will be here and that in turn they will want us to visit each of their houses and have a bite to eat and a drink while everyone else watches on. This hospitable ritual can take hours and can be somewhat trying when you are unable to speak the language.

"I think we had better move on," says Lee, I agree but it is easier said than done. We stand up and say many 'thank yous' and then walk onto the street hoisting our rucksacks onto our backs. We continue to walk to the edge of the village with a dozen children following behind us laughing and shouting "English, English!" They gradually drop away until we think we have shaken them off. This is the sort of road where you might get two cars a day if you are lucky, though in reality they are more likely to be tractors. Then we hear a commotion behind us that causes us to turn round to see a dozen or so people and a donkey hurrying towards us.

"Now what?" asks Lee, and we both look at each other puzzled. The little crowd soon catches up and with them all talking at once; they gesticulate to us to take our rucksacks off. Then two of the men rope the rucksacks either side of the donkey's saddle. I see they are concerned about us carrying our bags.

"Maybe, but what do we do with the donkey when we get a lift?" asks Lee.

"Looks like this is our lift and I reckon we will be in Greece forever. It will take us weeks to reach the next town at this pace".

We both know it will be no good attempting to explain. A mother in a headscarf comes up to us with a piece of paper with a few words of Greek written on it, which she gives to Lee. Then with a short branch broken from a tree she switches the donkey's butt and then puts the branch in my hand. The donkey trots off down the road and we pursue our baggage to the cheers of villagers who wave us on our way. We follow the donkey and as there is only one road, there's not a lot of choice. Lee is not too pleased that we have been burdened with a beast of burden. At least my back appreciates the rest and my legs feel a lot lighter. We are used to walking and I am happy to do so but previously there has always been the expectation of a lift in the not too distant future. Now the length of walk ahead of us is unknown. Even though it is October the sun is still strong and the walking keeps us reaching for the water bottle.

After a couple of hours we think we will sit and rest for a while; however, the donkey is reluctant to stop. I am used to handling horses, I was brought up with pit ponies and cart horses and they were trained to do as you bid, but this donkey is something else. He has a rope bridle, a wooden saddle and a thick head; there is no rein or lead and we do not know the Greek commands. Lee gets one side of his head I get the other and with both our hands on his bridle we pull him to a standstill. Now he is still, we go and sit on the grassy bank at the side of the track. There is no means of tethering the donkey and no sooner have we sat down than he starts to trot off down the road. So we have to jump up and chase after him in order to keep tabs on our baggage.

Michael Benton

The donkey is always in the lead and he obviously knows the way; though we do wonder when a little later he departs from the road, jumps onto a sheep track and takes off up the hillside. A few hundred yards later we can see from our hillside vantage that he has taken a short cut, which has saved us about half a mile.

We seem to have been walking all day, we have seen no cars and we are getting hungry and tired. Then we notice a village in the distance and the donkey quickens his pace. We are relieved and looking forward to a good rest. Following the donkey into the village, he trots into a backyard and quenches his thirst at a stone water trough. We untie our bags and take them off the saddle. People start to come out of the house and the donkey is led away. Lee gives the note to the lady of the house and she nods enthusiastically, ushering us into the house to a meal of meatballs, olives and Ouzo.

When we have eaten, Lee and I decide we need some peace and quiet. While in the village we would be continuously viewed and talked at, and would struggle to understand everybody's gestures. So we plan to say our thanks and goodbyes, then slip out into the night. We could then pitch our tent in a sheltered spot in the valley below. We eventually succeed in escaping the bewildered villagers and rest our weary bodies in the quiet of the night.

The next morning we wake up rather late, as usual. We leave the tent and its contents and make our way back into the village to look for breakfast. At the bakery we are given bread and a glass of wine! This is not normal practice. Everyone is bustling about, covered trays are leaving the bakery and it is not at all like the usual slow pace of village life. The Greeks have a frequently used saying "cigar, cigar", which means "slowly, slowly" and the atmosphere is definitely not "cigar, cigar". Then a man beckons us across the street. The Greeks do not call you with a hooked finger as we might in England but use the whole hand in a downward movement, which at first glance might be interpreted as a dismissive action to go away. We cross the road and are invited into the restaurant and offered another glass of wine. The tables have cloths on them with vases of fresh flowers. Something different is going on; perhaps another Saints Day? They seem to have one every week here. I try to enquire of the restaurant owner what is going on, and he excitedly tries to tell us while rubbing both his forefingers vigorously together. Ah, a wedding, now it is making sense, maybe we should leave, but on making for the door we are called back to the table and given another glass of wine. Lee thinks it is a bit early in the day but he is not complaining.

By the time we have finished the next glass the street is filling with people and then a family come out from the back of the restaurant. We step into the street which is now filling up with villagers and we can see a group of men walking towards us shaking hands and kissing the folk as they pass through the crowd. This looks like the groom and his entourage. They shake our hands and pass on by and then we follow the throng along the street until we come to the little stone church. The groom's party stand on the church steps and the bell starts to ring out. They are looking up the road in the opposite direction from where they came. After some minutes another group forms further along the street around a girl in a full-skirted white dress with her maids and relatives all smartly dressed. They walk sedately along the road towards the church, the Papas then ushers the groom and his party into the church. Lee and I stay outside with the lesser villagers who clap the bride and her family into the church.

The bell stops ringing, the chanting and singing starts. The ceremony seems to go on for a very long time. People peer through the door and some go in and come out again but it is dark inside and we cannot see what is happening. We sit on the steps under the warm sun and wait patiently.

Eventually people start to come out, then the bride and groom appear in the doorway to cheers and shouts. Music strikes up, one man with a lute and another with a fiddle and they escort the couple along the street to the restaurant with all the villagers following behind.

On reaching the restaurant the couple, followed by their families, go inside and take their seats at the main table. We are given seats by the door with yet more wine. Then the little dishes of food start to circulate, meatballs, stuffed fig leaves, goat chops and rice, followed by melon, grapes and sweets, with of course more wine.

It isn't just the people who enjoy the wedding; the village cats and dogs have a field day. The cats sit under the tables and in hideouts watching like hawks for any dropped food upon which they can pounce and then retreat back to their vantage point. The dogs wander, constantly prowling for bigger things; left over chop bones are a particular bounty that gives rise to the occasional scrap between the scavengers.

After we have all eaten, the musicians go back into the street and resume playing. Now the dancing starts with the happy couple on their own in the centre and everybody else forming a circle around them. We are each given a white handkerchief and then joining hands, we circle the couple like a giant 'ring-a-ring-a-roses'. We circle, twirl and wave our hankies in great merriment. My straw hat becomes of interest and suddenly it becomes a hat dance where it circulates from head to head going up into the air between each transfer. One of the bridesmaids takes a fancy to my hat and tries to retain it and when the other dancers indicate she should pass it on she declines. When complaints and attempts to snatch become too numerous she breaks out of the ring and crosses over to me placing it on my head with a shriek of laughter. As she lowers her hand she runs her fingers through my beard with a further shriek followed by laughter from all around the ring. My beard is often a point of interest in Greece. Greek men are always clean-shaven except for the priests who all have bushy untrimmed beards. So people are always asking me if I am a Papas.

The dancing continues and I notice this particular young lady is frequently trying to negotiate her position so that she can dance next to me. The idea of the hankie is to wave like a little flag and also for partners to grasp easily when they are re-linking hands. However, this young lady would noticeably grasp my hand as well as the hankie and was being quite vigorous with her dance. She is a good little dancer about a head shorter than me and in her late teens or early twenties. She has dark shoulder length hair and dark black sparkling eyes. She dances like a gazelle and seems to be everywhere and doing her best to attract everybody's attention. But her efforts do not go un-noticed by Lee who reckons my luck will be in tonight, but to keep a weather eye open for her dad. At the next pause in the dance she pulls me by the sleeve down the side of a shop on the pretext of Ouzo. Once out of the gaze of the partygoers she twiddles my beard and giggles, I guess beards are a new experience for her and a moment later she is stroking it with her face. She gives me a quick kiss on the cheek and then off we go again around to the back of the shop where we collapse on an old sofa by the back door. She is a lively girl though fumbling and nervous. Neither of us knows what to expect of the other and while we lie reclining on the sofa I hear Lee's voice calling down the entry saying they are looking for us and to come back to the party. We are on our feet in a flash; Lee the marine had spotted us slip away. The girl pulls me away from the direction of Lee's voice and around the other side of the shop. Pushing me back into the street she then withdraws back down the entry. We all continue dancing and drinking until almost dark when people seem to dwindle. The dancers become fewer and the music slower. We gather that now the bride and groom have gone the party is over, so Lee and I saunter back to our tent to relax after a very different day.

We lay in the tent musing over the day's events with Lee quizzing me about what I didn't get up to with the Greek girl. We plan that tomorrow we should move further along this very slow road. After a couple of hours the music and singing starts up again. It sounds almost Oriental with the drift of the wind. Lee reckons the party has resumed again and we should return for more dancing and more wine. I think he fancies one of the other bridesmaids but he keeps saying she is too young for him. Well, we decide to return and find two parties going on, the bride and her family are feasting and dancing at one end of the village, and the groom and his relatives at a house at the other end of the village. The majority of villagers are now linked arm-in-arm in lines, and are walking and singing along the main street between the two houses. When they reach one house they turn and walk back to the other. There are half a dozen of these lines of people and when they come face to face they stop and chat and some people swap lines. We watch this with interest; it seems to be a form of a courtship process with particularly lively interaction amongst some of the youngsters. This slow line dancing seems to go on forever. Suddenly the houses open their doors and more trays of food are brought out. More meat, bread, olives and now Ouzo. Ouzo is a Greek spirit, clear like water but very strong, some people drink it neat and others take it with water. When water is added it turns cloudy and looks like skimmed milk but tastes like firewater. This is a sign of serious celebration and the dancing starts up once more with everybody seeming to be revitalised.

There does not seem to be any sign of the bridesmaid. Perhaps dad had got wind of her adventures and she is being kept indoors. Lee is pleased about that as he thinks the two of us could get into trouble and it might end up in a brawl with her brothers.

"You spoke too soon Lee here she comes carrying sweet pastries and a bottle of Ouzo."

She has changed out of her bridesmaid dress into day clothes. Looking older and not quite so pretty but still sparkling and full of energy, she unloads the goodies into our hands. I have never known Lee to refuse any form of food or drink. Then her friend, the other bridesmaid appears with more goodies. We have never eaten or drunk so much since arriving in Greece. The four of us return to the street dancing but we are so full and unsteady on our feet that Lee and I spend more time sitting out watching the others. Our two bridesmaid friends dance in front of us and repeatedly return to sit for a moment and chat before returning to dance. I learn that my particular girl is called Sofia and she wants to learn English. I do not think that is what she was trying to say earlier. Lee is adamant that we both stay in the street. He thinks that if we go missing again it could end in family retribution or worse.

"Worse?" I say,

"Yes, another wedding tomorrow, and only today's leftovers for the wedding breakfast." I reckon he just doesn't fancy his bridesmaid. After a further hour of dance and Ouzo, Lee and I could hardly stand and decide to return to the tent. We take formal leave of our lady hosts with a kiss and then make off in the general direction of the tent. It is very dark and our heads are swimming. All the tree trunks look the same and nothing looks familiar. All of a sudden I feel my stomach come into my mouth. You know that funny feeling when you go over a hump back bridge. I am in freefall but only for a couple of seconds before I hit the ground and crumple into a ball. I do not know what has happened then I hear Lee calling,

"Mike, Mike where are you? Stop mucking about, where have you gone? Are you okay?"

I can hear his voice way above me,

"I think I'm okay",

But then I heave and lose my wedding feast.

The food and the drink combined with the fall over a cliff of some fifteen feet was the last straw. I'm stunned and senseless, my feet are

Mad Dogs and an Englishman

tingling. Have I broken my back or my legs? What is wrong? I do not know which way up I am. With Lee's help I manage to stand and can just about bear my weight through my legs. I am very lucky I have not broken a leg but I guess I was so relaxed when I hit the ground the Ouzo must have saved me from serious injury. At least Lee avoided walking off the same cliff. Eventually we locate the tent, fall in and sleep well into the next day.

On rising I check out my body, which is stiff and bruised but no serious damage seems to have occurred. We pack the tent and struggle back to the village, which we have to pass through on the road for Athos. Passing the bakery we buy a loaf of bread and receive a piece of Feta cheese. As we walk along the road the children come out and gather around us. One of them must have gone to tell Sofia we were on the move. She joins us and insists we go to her house for a cup of tea and say farewell to her family. While we sit drinking tea with her mother she disappears only to return a little later with a donkey. You should have seen Lee's face,

"Not another bloody mule!" Well our bags are strapped onto the saddle and we are waved off by half of the village. This time Sofia leads the donkey and it is evident she is coming with us. She walks along side constantly smiling, as happy as Lee is sullen.

"I think you are stuck with this girl, she has probably got her passport tucked in her pocket". Sofia laughs though she does not have the slightest idea what has been said. We are walking at a fair pace and my legs are really aching. After a couple of hours we take a rest and Sofia cuts open a melon, which is most welcome. Continuing on our way we eventually reach the village of Palaiochori. This is apparently as far as the donkey is going and we are taken into a house for refreshment. Sofia disappears again while we are eating and returns later with a man who speaks a little English. He is a lumberjack cutting timber in the vicinity and he says he can take us tomorrow in his truck to Athos. Until then we can stay with Sofia's relatives in one of their upstairs rooms. It is a usual Greek evening with strained efforts of conversation lubricated with Ouzo. Some fellow comes to sing to us with a one-stringed triangular banjo. This eases things a little as we do not feel we have to talk while he is performing. We are almost asleep when bedtime is indicated and we are shown to our room. We sleep on our sleeping bags on the bare boards.

During the night I stir and feel a body on my right side but when I fell asleep Lee was on my left side. Feeling around I find that there are two Lees, only there can't be. Sofia must have crept into the room. I try to explore what I take to be Sofia when a finger is pressed against my lips followed by her hot lips. Then she takes my hand and places it onto her breast. She is very quiet and calm now making slow and gentle movements whilst I fall asleep. When I next stir it is dawn and Sofia has gone. I could not quite grasp this, had she really been there or had it all been a dream? Lee is snoring soundly and oblivious to every thing. I lie there quietly waiting for sounds to tell me the household is awake. At the first kitchen noise I am up and investigating the day.

The lady of the house is brewing and cleaning she says "good morning" and gives me a glass of water. I drink it and go to look around outside. Sofia is coming down the street with her arms full of bread. She smiles innocently and exchanges a cheery "kalimera" (good morning). We all sit down to breakfast of fresh bread and gruel, something like peanut butter. While we are eating a truck stops outside and the lumberjack comes in. It is all systems go. Sofia's donkey is also waiting outside almost hidden by a huge load of firewood destined for her village. Sofia is no longer smiling and looks at the sky, and then me muttering some words she hugs me intensely and plants a kiss on each check. Then she pushes a scrap of paper in my hand. I look at it but it is in Greek of course.

"It's her address for when you come back". the lumberjack says.

"Oh, but we do not expect to come back this way".

The lumberjack looked at Sofia and then at me and says

"If you love her you come back".

I feel terrible but we have to climb in the truck. I can only look and wave as Sofia, the donkey and the villagers disappear behind clouds of dust from the truck.

We are on our way to Athos, which is the eastern peninsular of the three fingers pointing down from Salonika. We are making good time in the truck, winding our way through the picturesque mountains until we reach the village of Nea Rhoda where our driver drops us. The village does not take much checking out. On finding the teahouse

Mad Dogs and an Englishman

we sit and review our plans. It looks like a narrow wild track now onto Athos, but the teahouse man is saying no to the track. After some further attempts to communicate he goes off to fetch a man who can speak English. He is a doctor who explains that it is impossible to go by land onto Athos. We have to go back a village and cross by sea, however we are told we need a Visa for Athos as it is a separate State and we need to obtain it from the Consul in Salonika. A boat takes pilgrims over once a week and life there is very different. There are twenty-four monasteries and you can stay one night at each free of charge. Only men are allowed and no female of any species, so no hens, cows or female goats, which must make life very difficult.

Years ago there were thousands of Greek Orthodox monks but at this time there are only about fifteen hundred, who are now mainly recruited from Russia as the Greeks no longer show an interest. They make a meagre living by trading in olives, wine and fire wood to the main land. Their day consists of rising at two thirty in the morning to the sound of drumming on a plank of wood. They then pray until seven am when they have breakfast before turning out to work in the hills until their evening meal. Limited visitors are encouraged and expected to participate in the monastic life. Lee thinks it is as well that we do not have a Visa because seven days of austerity and work would be too much for him. So now what? Well we are advised to spend the night in an old monastery down the road, which now acts as a hotel and staging post for people waiting for the boat. It is very basic and still has the old cells with wooden benches, but it is only for one night and we are quite used to sleeping on bare boards.

The next morning we leave the monastic hotel and have to backtrack. For some miles we ride on a tractor, sitting on the wheel arches. Then we transfer onto a donkey cart, very slow and laborious along rocky tracks just a few feet wide. Along the side of the track there are a few conical thatched huts more like you would expect to find in Africa. By evening we arrive at a small village where I do not think any foreigners have been before. Everyone comes out to meet us, we are offered a meal while all the villagers stand around and watch. After we have eaten we are taken to what looks like a barn. It is constructed in wood and stone with the door hanging off. Inside are some chairs in a row and an ancient barbers chair in front of a bench. It must be an abandoned barbers shop. No, we are told it is the dentist's office and we can stay there because he is in Salonika. When we are alone I investigate the drawers in the bench. There are boxes of anaesthetic phials, rusty pliers and probes. It is absolutely filthy and looks like it was abandoned fifty years ago, but for us it is shelter for the night.

The next morning a man who speaks reasonably good English comes to find us. He is a farmer from Drama, a wealthy man for those parts. He says he has three farms and is looking forward to coming to college in England next year. He would like to take us in his car to show us his farms and of course his family. We agree if he is going in the right direction.

"Oh yes surely" and so we spend the next two days visiting his farms and inspecting his produce and hearing him repeatedly say how happy he is. At the end of the second day he takes us to the town of Kavala on the main coast road.

He bids us farewell in Kavala, which is a big town with traffic, something we have not seen for a long time. Just before dusk an American guy and his wife in a brand new VW estate wagon pick us up. So much space, comfort and speed. Turkey here we come.

Chapter Three

Gateway to Asia

The comfort of the new Volkswagen is unbelievable compared with our previous modes of transport. We are now covering more ground in an hour than previously in a day. The road is smooth and wide, although the continuous columns of Greek army trucks full of soldiers hinder us a little.

By nightfall we have crossed the border into Turkey and booked into a hotel in Edirne. After eating we sit and chat mainly about our travels and ourselves. Our driver is Rami, he is in his thirties and of Afro-Caribbean decent. He works as a photographer for the National Geographic magazine and tours the world looking for photographic stories. His lady companion is Mel, of similar age, and she is a white American from California. Their mission is to travel to the little known territory of Hunza in the Himalayas where people live to the grand old age of a hundred and twenty years. Rami has a vision of doing a full feature for the magazine. He has three expensive cameras and all sorts of equipment worth thousands of pounds, which we help him carry into the hotel rather than risk leaving them in the car overnight. We continue to talk into the early hours about our travel experiences and Rami tells us about his last feature on Zen Buddhism in Japan. We eventually retire to our rooms and fall asleep on comfortable beds, in more comfort than I have experienced since Chateauneuf.

At breakfast next morning Rami and Mel say they are happy for us to travel with them to Istanbul and that suits Lee and I just fine. We spend most of the day in the car and enjoy the drive through to Istanbul, a very big city where the traffic is chaotic. Cars drive anywhere and everywhere, the vehicles line up six abreast, honking horns and jumping from one line to another. Rami does not know what to do or where to go, so he simply follows the car in front and just drives around the city while we view the sights. None of us have seen anything quite like this before, just a sheer car jungle. He spots a big building with Hilton on it.

"That will do" he says and drives through the gate. Oh yes we are going up in the world now but Lee and I cannot afford this splendour. Rami says,

"Ok, you two go and find a room and then come back here to eat". He and Mel book into the Hilton and Lee and I take to the street to search for a hotel to suit our pockets. We find a two star hotel some five hundred yards away. It is basic but secure. On returning to the Hilton, Rami and Mel have had food brought to their room, which they share with us while we plan the next few days in the big city.

The following morning I go on my own to the British Consulate to collect my post. On showing my passport they give me a letter from home and a form from customs asking me to collect a parcel. I sit down to read the news from England. The old man from next door has died. The local newspaper is looking for a story and photos. Mom and Dad have received the films from France and Italy and they are ok but I should try not to move so fast. They have put three films in the post for Istanbul, so that's probably the package to be collected from customs.

I buy a map of the city and enquire as to the way. Eventually I find myself on what looks like an industrial estate near the docks. A local lad walks with me to a huge warehouse of a building with an armed guard on the door. I show him the customs form and he waves me through. On approaching the desk I am asked for my passport and the customs man disappears into the back office. Looking around I see all sorts of crates and boxes, stacked in various piles in this huge hanger. The man returns with a packet on which I recognise my mother's handwriting and I can see the packet has been opened. He tips three boxes of film onto the counter and whilst speaking in Turkish he attempts to open the film case to which I object. He persists so I put my hand on his and say, "No".

He responds angrily in Turkish but the only word I recognise is film. Now he asks me for money, for the duty I expect. So I take some Lira out and put it on the counter. He looks puzzled and then points to the camera hanging on my shoulder. He motions to put the camera on the counter, which I do. He then takes the camera; the films and passport back into his office and tells me to sit on the chair by the door. I sit and wait for about twenty minutes and then I return to the counter and call for the officer. He comes out and points to the chair. I am fed up with waiting and ask for my passport and camera and try to indicate I will come back another time. He ignores me so I repeat "Passport and camera" knowing that he knows these words. He looks anxious so I shout

"Passport and camera", he then rings a bell by the counter and the gun-totting soldier comes in. They exchange a few words and then the soldier takes my arm and leads me to the other side of the warehouse. We arrive at what I can only describe as a wire cage, a ten-foot wire cube with a door in it. I am put inside and the door is locked. I am locked up in a cage like a zoo animal. Is this what they do to tourists in Turkey? Every ten minutes or so I call out but I am totally ignored and the place now appears to be deserted. After an hour or so I give up and lie down on the wire floor.

It is about five hours later when a man in a suit walks across the concrete floor to the cage with my passport in his hand.

"Mr Benton, my officer tells me you have been difficult so he has called me while I am on holiday to sort out this matter because he does not want to keep you here all night."

"Well that is good of him but I just want to collect my belongings and go."

"It is not that simple. If you behave we can go to my office and talk." So I agree, he lets me out and we walk to his office. He gives me a cup of water and we sit down. He then goes on to explain in excellent English that a permit is required to bring unexposed film into Turkey. The customs man can only release the film to me if I have a permit, as unopened film is a security risk. I try to explain that I need new film to photograph the wonderful sights in Istanbul. He tells me I can buy good photos and postcards of the sights very cheaply.

"However, security is very, very important. Turkey is almost on the verge of war with Greece." I had seen the army columns and tanks all along the road from the border to Istanbul.

"Well I should confiscate and destroy the film and your camera then hand you over to the army in case you are a spy. However, I do not think you are a spy, I think you are too young and you are English, but I have to make sure you are not a security problem. So I am being very good to you, if you agree to open your camera and give me the film inside."

I agree, he gives me the camera and asks me to open it, which I do and when he sees there is no film he says

"Good you can close it. Now it is a serious offence to be found with any camera near any military zone. If you are found in such an area you will be arrested and go to prison. So instead of confiscating your camera I will just disarm it."

He takes the camera, pulls open the clockwork handle and forces it back until it breaks off. He hands me the camera and the handle saying.

"You can get a new handle in England. Now the films I will have to return to the sender in England. Here is your passport, please keep away from the military zones. You are free to go."

I am somewhat stunned but no longer of a mind to protest. As I hastily leave the customs office, the man at the desk glares at me and the guard at the door gives a faint smile.

Having been so long away from my companions I make straight back to the Hilton to tell the other three of my experience. When I tell them about the camera Rami looks horrified.

"Oh no, I have thousands of dollars worth of equipment. Keeping it secure from robbers is one thing but the army as well, what can I do?"

We decide that it would be best to keep the equipment locked in a suitcase in the hotel and just take his small camera out into town. After packing his equipment away we walk into town to be tourists.

Most of our time we spend in the huge Bazaar (sook), where you can buy practically anything. At the top end there are the gold and jewellery shops, silks, furs and inlaid furniture and at the bottom end rusty tools and car parts. I find a metal worker who I show my broken camera to. He looks, nods and proceeds to make a new pin to fit the winding handle back onto the camera and all accomplished in less than ten minutes. I am very pleased with the job and for a few Lira my camera is now operational. I dare not think what the customs man would say.

Now, since you can buy anything here I enquire about a film for my restored camera. A young lad of about six or seven years takes us through the winding alleys to a camera shop. The owner gives us all a furtive look, opens the camera and says,

"Yes, expensive".

He goes into the back of the shop and returns with a Kodak Super 8 film, which he fits into the camera. The cost is about four pounds, three times what I would pay in England but I have no choice. Rami and I try to take photos in and around the bazaar. I took one of a man carrying a six-cylinder car engine on his back and other extraordinary sights, but some of the time the people object and try to stop us filming. Then a pickpocket tries to snatch my passport but the attached string stops him getting away with it.

Istanbul is full of mosques and every few hours there is a relay of calls from the various Imams praying to Allah. Sometimes they are so close we jump with surprise unaware we are just below a minaret. There is so much to see in Istanbul it can take weeks to see the many sights, so sometimes we split up, Lee and I usually stay together though occasionally we do our own thing. After a couple of days Rami and Mel move from the Hilton to the Park hotel, just as nice but cheaper and Lee and I feel more at home when we are visiting them there for our showers and snacks.

One night we all decide to go out for a meal. We drive along the Bosphorus until we come to a restaurant that we all like and decide to go in. We sit eating for over three hours, some of the food I can recognise, liver, aubergines and beans garnished with tomatoes, olives and lettuce leaves, followed by fish and melon washed down with Raki of course. Raki is the Turkish version of the Greek Ouzo. Another night we go to a nightclub, or should I say several! Entertainment is traditional dancing by men and women; the highlight being the floorshow of belly dancing, which is quite amusing with the various gyrations and contortions. Though I personally think the ladies are rather plump and some excessively so.

We continue with our trips and visits day after day for a couple of weeks or more. One day we go to see the Aya Sofia (the Blue Mosque) and museum, an impressive building originally built as a church at the time of Constantine. It was rededicated as a mosque when Constantinople became Istanbul following the Ottoman invasion. Another day we are on the hillside suburbs among such poverty it is difficult to believe this is the same city. In some places we feel insecure when on our own and feel more and more the need to keep in a group. We meet an Australian who has just had his motorcycle stolen while he was standing by it. Another man had his watch stolen off his wrist. I myself had a five-pound travellers cheque snatched out of my hand while queuing in a bank. One never knows what to expect next in this city. Rami and Mel become quite fearful of being robbed and do not like to go out without Lee and myself as escort. Then we hear that two hitchhikers have been robbed and killed on the road to Ankara. Rami is now having second thoughts about continuing with his journey east. Mel suggests that if Lee and I travel with them they would be more secure and we would all be safer as a group. We all agree that this is probably for the best.

So to celebrate our new campaign to Hunza we decide to have one last night out on the town before we drive to the interior. Mel phones a friend who she met on a visit seven years ago to enquire about a good club. He is a wealthy and influential Turk who comes around to the hotel in no time and whisks us off to a top club to see the best acts and bellies in town, all at his expense. There we are all enjoying the evening when I notice Rami has gone quiet and beads of sweat are forming on his forehead. I ask him if he is okay. He says he feels hot and itchy and then his face goes a grey colour. Mel says, "I think it is his diabetes, he has eaten something to upset him". She decides to go back to their hotel with her Turkish friend to get his tablets. No sooner had they left than Rami becomes delirious and collapses onto the floor. His face is now bloated and his pulse light and rapid and then he loses consciousness. I put him in the recovery position and the manager calls for a taxi. Lee, the manager and I struggle to get Rami into the car and the driver takes us to hospital. On arrival Rami vomits after being carried out of the taxi and placed onto a trolley. The doctors and nurses speak no English and are perplexed by his condition. I can only tell them that he is diabetic and has a cardiac condition. They set up a drip, take blood and give him an injection. Meanwhile Mel has collected his tablets and is driving around town with her Turkish friend trying to find which hospital we are in. It is two o'clock in the morning when a distraught Mel manages to find us and we are all around Rami's bedside. He is now motionless but breathing steadily with an occasional long breath. He does not respond to us talking to him but I think he can hear us. I dare not say what I am thinking. The doctor says he is stable but he cannot say any more for now other than,

"We will see tomorrow".

If anything happens to Rami we have a distraught Mel, a Volkswagen and all sorts of things to sort out in a foreign country and I just do not know where to start. I just keep thinking he must pull through. I guess Lee is thinking the same as he keeps trying to say

"What if?"

Lee and I leave Mel at Rami's bedside and walk back to our hotel. Mel knows where to find us if she needs us, otherwise we will return in the morning. The next day on returning to hospital Rami is sitting up in bed and appears well and clear headed. Mel has gone for breakfast and a doctor who speaks good English comes to tell us Rami is a very lucky man. Arriving half an hour later he would probably have died. For now he is okay, although they would like to keep him for another day before discharge. Now we can all make jokes and tease Rami for causing everyone so much trouble.

Following discharge from hospital Rami is feeling somewhat vulnerable to the extent that he is considering calling the whole trip off. We are heading into remote areas, the vast deserts of Iraq and Iran, the remote mountains of Pakistan and Afghanistan. There will be no hospitals for hundreds of miles and Rami's life has just been saved simply because he was in a city with a good hospital at hand. A couple of days further on in the mountains of Turkey, he would have undoubtedly died. The experience has bonded the four of us together in complete trust and interdependence. I think it is Mel who started to think about desert nomads and the tribesmen of the Khyber. She thinks we should be armed and prepared for the unexpected. Maybe she is thinking what might happen to her as a defenceless western woman. So we go to the bazaar to the bottom end and find a gun shop. Rami and Lee are looking at German pistols; they both agree that the same chunky one with a magazine in the handle would be suitable for them. While they go out the back of the shop and try them out in a heap of sand Mel and I look around the shop. I am not too happy about carrying a gun; I know nothing about guns other than shotguns, which are completely different. Anyway I have no money for a gun. Mel says she will pay for it as it is in her interests. Rami and Lee return to listen to our debate, then Rami says,

"Why not get a gas gun. That will not kill anyone and it may be useful in some situations to disable an attacker".

"Okay I can live with that", I say.

The shopkeeper then shows me a small six chambered 9mm revolver, which fires small metal cartridges with a yellow wax-like substance instead of a bullet. It also has a screw-on flare attachment for the end of the barrel. It comes with its own little holster with a button down flap that fits neatly onto my belt. The shopkeeper takes me outside to try it, the trigger is very light and it gives a loud bang followed by a wisp of smoke. We go back inside the shop to escape the gas and complete our purchases. I thread the holster onto my belt and position it left front. It is small and compact and well hidden under my jumper but easily accessible for my right hand. I feel a bit like a bandit with a gun and a knife on my belt. The knife is my old scout sheath knife, which I keep on my belt at the back just to the left of my spine. It never gets in the way there except when I lie down and then I take it out and put it under my pillow. I never think of my knife as a weapon. It is a tool for cutting string, carving tent pegs, cutting up food and opening tin cans.

When I think of the knife debate these days I wonder where it all went wrong. I first had my knife when I was ten years old. It was for holidays and weekends in the woods. I would never think of taking it to school, it would be out of place and unnecessary. In the 1950`s all the lads had sheath knives and wore them openly. It was part of the scout uniform and no one thought anything was amiss if a lad had a knife on is belt. It is not the knife that is the problem it is the thinking. When did it become a weapon instead of a tool?

Anyway I digress. We leave the shop armed to the teeth and ready for the deserts of Arabia and the mountains of Afghanistan. Our motives for carrying guns are purely defensive, but it is not just aggressive tribesmen we need to be wary of, there are also wild wolves out there to contend with. We also buy tins and packets of food from a store before returning to the hotel. We then have a good night's sleep before resuming our travels into Asia the following morning.

As planned, we leave Istanbul along the main central highway for the capital Ankara. The city is very small as far as capitals go; it was chosen by Ataturk, the political father of Turkey, because of its central location. A new city was built to house the government and its new administration in the 1920's. We make it to Ankara in two days, though the driving seems to be getting too much for Rami and so Lee and I take turns at the wheel. Rami wants to rest for a few days in a hotel. Lee and I cannot afford such continuous luxuries so we sleep in the back of the estate car. The days are spent visiting ancient Hittite ruins and museums. In the evenings we frequent the restaurants and bars, eating and drinking while Rami recuperates. Privately, Lee and I have concerns about Rami being physically up to the pressure of travelling in the remote areas we are heading for. There is also his reluctance to 'rough it', even to the point of making detours or even backtracking in order to reach a hotel for the night. After a few days Rami is ready to proceed and we set off on the main road east for Erzerum. We are now in high mountains with falling snow, which is getting deeper by the hour. The roads are treacherous, narrow and winding around the mountains. There is a sheer drop off to one side often to hundreds of feet below. There are no safety barriers and particularly on left hand bends you can see no road in front, just fresh air and a great drop, with the remains of vehicles the size of dinky cars lying broken at the bottom of the valley. Mile after mile it is like looking down on a linear scrap yard. I remember thinking you would not know if you went over until you had that sinking feeling in your stomach and saw the cliff face rushing upwards past the window. To go off this road is certain death and there is no possibility of recovery. Even helicopters could not reach into these ravines; my thoughts were interrupted by the fact that we had come to a standstill. As we turn the last bend we see the snow has drifted to the height of the car and now it is impossible to go any further, so we have to reverse along this treacherous road for about half a mile until we have sufficient space on the road to do a ten-point turn. After back tracking for some miles we come to a mountain teahouse. It is little more than one of the wooden shacks situated along the roadside every few hours purely to give refreshment and rest to travellers. Inside they have an oil burning stove with seats and benches encircling it. The stoves give off ferocious heat and they roar continuously, so you end up with a burnt face and knees and a frozen back. We all sit and drink our tea from the usual hourglass-shaped vessels, presented on a tin saucer holding a couple of chunks of rock sugar. The custom is that you put a lump of sugar in your mouth and then sip the hot tea through it. The sugar does not immediately dissolve like a western sugar lump would but it stays in your mouth like a boiled sweet. Having finished our tea we enquire about a bed for the night as darkness is falling.

We are escorted up the hill behind the teahouse to a picturesque little house. The wooden stairway is on the outside of the building and leads to three small wooden-planked rooms. Lee and I take one room and Rami and Mel another. Inside are two wooden cots with a very thin, stiff mattress and a thick cotton cover on each. The cots are so short we have to sleep with our feet through the gaps between the rails in the footboard. Lee and I sleep well, but Rami and Mel are up most of the night, just wanting to get back on the road. In the morning the sun is shining brightly but the air is very cold, when you breath in, the cold air hits you between the eyes.

We consult the map and local opinion, and we are told we cannot go any further east due to the snow blocking the road. We can however take the road south via Kayseri and then onto Adana. Fortunately we are able to follow in the path of a snowplough, rather slow but safe. Stopping at a village for provisions we are mobbed by children calling for cigarettes and adults who stand at a safe distance and stare with curiosity. The women are dressed in black with brightly coloured adornments and gold jewellery. The men are dressed in woollen jackets, baggy trousers and cloth caps. Animals wander aimlessly around the village. It seems a very strange land with beauty and filth side by side. Rami takes his camera out to take some photos of village life. The children fight roughly with each other to get into where they imagine the centre of the photo will be. Order is not restored until we climb back into the car and drive away, though some of the children try to pursue us for yards along the road.

After some hours we descend from the frozen mountains to the slightly warmer plains and reach the ancient town of Antakya. Now it is Mel's turn to be taken ill, we suspect food poisoning from the symptoms, so we need to park up again until she recovers. We find a hotel suitable for Rami and Mel though not to their usual standard, meanwhile Lee and I have use of the car to explore the region during the day and to sleep in at night.

Syria is now in our sights mainly because it is the only road open to us. We are looking forward to warmer weather and less treacherous roads.

Chapter Four

The Road to the Holy Land

On leaving the ancient town of Antakya we drive leisurely along a winding road to the Syrian border. The Turkish / Syrian border is disputed and patrolled by both sides. Every town has a passport control and every foreigner is repeatedly checked through. In addition to the Kurdish infiltrators there is the cold war with Israel and the possibility of travellers trying to gain access to Israel via Syria, which is strictly forbidden. Some Westerners have two passports, one with Israeli visas and one without, because you are not allowed into or through an Arab country if you have an Israeli visa in your passport.

At the border I am the one to be selected by the guard as the mostly likely looking Jew

"I think if I search your luggage I will find a passport for Israel" he says and starts to probe my bag.

"No I have just come to see Damascus and the sights", I reply.

He soon gives up and lets us pass. Having just recovered from that ordeal we are cruising along a nice stretch of straight road when Rami spots a petrol station. Being very low on fuel he swings off the road rather suddenly and skids across the shale forecourt. There are two armed soldiers at the station who immediately jump into action and as we come to a standstill we find one either side of us with rifles pointed, one at Rami and the other at Mel. The points of the bayonets are scraping the glass of the windows. The soldiers then take a pace back and indicate to us to get out. We are lined up against the filling station kiosk by the one soldier, while the other checks over the contents of the car. We hold our breath and silently give each other sideways glances. The soldiers are shouting aggressively at us and at each other as if they are angry that it is not a real attack. I think we are lucky they did not shoot first and check us over after. When they are finally satisfied that we are only foreign tourists and not raiders we are allowed to fill up with petrol and proceed on our way. When we reach the next town we decide we have had enough excitement for one day so we try to book into a hotel. However, trade must be a bit slow as a fight breaks out between three of the hoteliers as to who is going to take us in. This is all too much for us so we get back in the car and leave them brawling in the street. We drive onto the next town, which is Homs. Rami and Mel find a hotel that suits them without disrupting the neighbourhood and Lee and I bed down in the back of the estate wagon.

The countryside in Syria is very different; the land is much more flat, with gently rolling hills. It is very dry and dusty, with little grass and very few trees. We pass through small villages made up of small square huts painted brown, yellow and white. The people are really poor, wearing little more than rags and having long, unkempt hair. Donkeys and camels roam freely around the villages. Sheep and goats graze randomly over the desert like black ants under a roasting sun.

Damascus turns out to be more civilised, and everywhere its history can be seen. We are drawn to the sights and the cameras come out. There is the window in the house where St. Paul was lowered in a basket by Annanias to escape the Jews, which was later turned into a church and is now partly covered in debris from centuries of neglect. We visit the Omiyat mosque, the second largest in the world; it contains the tombs of Saladin and St John the Baptist, unbelievably lying side by side. There is so much to see we are overwhelmed and unaccustomed to the heat. We call at the American library thinking we will find a cool sanctuary. There we are shown a film about John F Kennedy and another about Syria's place in the world. We are then invited to stay for a traditional Syrian dinner. The next day we drive on for Lebanon.

Leaving Syria is fine but entering Lebanon is very frustrating. It appears Rami does not have a Carnet de Passage (passport) for the car. So it has to be impounded in Beirut docks. There is a charge to be escorted to the pound where the car is locked up and we are placed in a hotel. Rami then contacts the American Embassy and they explain that he needs to put up a bond of fifteen hundred dollars and pay some other fees to have the car released. This he arranges to do the next day and we all go to the docks and after much hassle drive the car out of the pound and take to the road for Tyre and Sidon.

Now another obstacle confronts us: 'The Military Zone'. As the road passes through Israel we are not allowed to enter so we have to return north and spend another night in Beirut. In the evening we meet a Lebanese teacher who speaks excellent English. He tells us of the tensions building up in the country between the Christians and the Muslims, the overbearing pressure from Syria and the constant threat of invasion by Israel. It is difficult to take in what he is saying when the city looks so Western and wealthy. In the morning it is possible to go skiing in the mountains above and in the afternoon, enjoy the water sports and sunbathe on the beach. However, the horrors that he was telling us about were to come true some two years later and they still haunt the Lebanese people forty years on. The following day we return to Syria to try to take another route in our effort to reach the Holy Land.

While eating a good meal in Damascus we are told of the world shattering news that President Kennedy has been shot dead. Anyone who lived through that time can usually remember where they were and what they were doing when they heard the news. We were sitting in that Damascus restaurant but unfortunately the waiter could not speak English to tell us any details. On quizzing him further he went on to say;

"Harold Wilson is now King of England", which made us think the whole story was a big misunderstanding. After all it was only a few days ago that we were watching a film about the life of JFK. Now we are all numb with the news of his death and frustrated by not knowing how or why.

The following day we continue our drive on to Jordan and reach the capital Amman. We take a break on the banks of the river Jordan at a crossing point where a battered old sign indicates the spot where

Michael Benton

Jesus was baptised by John the Baptist. As we stretch our legs alongside the Jordan we meet a Jordanian Legionnaire who speaks English and he tells us something about the area. He takes us along to Qumran, which is where a shepherd boy found the Dead Sea Scrolls. We roam at our leisure and explore some of the caves on the lower levels. The cave where the Scrolls were found is high up on the hillside and only accessible to climbers with all the right gear. How a bare footed shepherd boy climbed up there I cannot imagine, unless there is a more accessible entrance elsewhere. Following our exploration of the ancient monastic town built in the rocks we go for a stroll alongside the Dead Sea. At thirteen hundred feet below sea level, it is excessively salty but Lee and I decided to have a bathe. However, we find the buoyancy of the water difficult to swim in. You can imagine what happens when the water gets in your eyes and up your nose. When we come out we dry off quickly in the warm air and find we are snow white. The salt has dried like a thin shell, which cracks when we move and can be picked off like thin white corn flakes. It then leaves a fine film still attached to the skin, which irritatingly takes a day or two to wear off.

We decide to move on to Jerusalem, a divided city at this time. The old walled city of the bible is in Jordan and little has changed there for two thousand years. This is where Lee and I were to be spending the next six weeks. On the other side of the dividing wall you can see modern Jerusalem from the ramparts. The large concrete business and residential blocks of modern Israel stretch to the western horizon dwarfing the ancient walled city. I feel privileged to see the old city where little has changed since the time of Christ; to live amongst the people and experience their small joys and great fears of which I will speak later. Lee and I are comfortable in the sanctuary of the old city and decide it will be a good place to spend the approaching Christmas. Mel and Rami are not so sure. Rami is still weak from his illness and is even now struggling with the primitive comfort of Jerusalem. We wonder how on earth he will cope in the wilds of Afghanistan. However, the north east road to Hunza is now blocked by the winter snows and will continue to be so for another four months. The four of us spend a couple of days visiting the various tourist sights such as the Garden of Gethsemane, the Holy Sepulchre and the Dome of the Rock. After a prolonged discussion, Rami and Mel decide they need to return to

Europe and civilisation to pass the winter. They intend to return to Beirut and ship the car to Italy or Spain and spend the winter there. We make plans to meet up again in Karachi in the spring to prepare for the trek up to Hunza. Lee and I have some reservations about them ever making it and bid them a sad farewell after some six weeks of constant and mutually beneficial company.

Lee and I feel rather lonely; our base, our mobile hotel has now gone. Now we need to find somewhere to sleep at night. We sit outside the city wall, on the roadside just below the Damascus Gate and ponder upon our situation. The sun is warm and the road is dusty, heavy wagons and overcrowded buses line the road with people and donkeys picking their way in between. It is rather like a market without stalls. Suddenly we look up from where a pair of shoes have come to a standstill in front of us to see a fair-haired European lad staring at us. Almost simultaneously we say,

"English?" I recognise his accent is similar to my own.

"From where?" I ask,

"Staffordshire" he replies.

"I know that but where exactly?" I enquire excitedly. It turns out that he lived just two villages away from my home. We had in fact been to the same junior school but could not remember each other; I expect there was a year or two between us. His name is Roger and he is just about to get on a bus for Jericho. Before he leaves he suggests we visit the Garden Tomb just up the road,

"Bear right at the Damascus Gate and follow the wall round until you reach a green metal door." He assured us we would find it a sanctuary, a good place to think and make decisions. Those are his parting words as he climbs on the Jericho bus. I am stunned, such a brief encounter with a stranger from whom I had lived only a few miles away, for most of my life and yet we had both travelled a quarter of the way around the world to meet face to face for just a few minutes. I reflected on this later and found the experience comparable to a passage from the Bible,

'And it came to pass that on the way to Jerusalem a stranger appeared on the road and pointed in the direction of the tomb'.

Chapter Five

The Garden Tomb

Wearily we climb the hill and follow our directions to the green door, a solid metal door all alone in a high stone wall that encircles the garden, which is the size of a small park. It looks like it could be a side door to a prison or a castle. We ring the bell and after a few minutes the door opens and we are invited in by a small lady who bids us put our heavy bags down by her house door. She invites us to enjoy the garden for a moment while she goes in doors. We wander and gaze at the lush tranquil garden. It is full of shrubs and trees, like a cultivated jungle. You cannot see the sky above for the foliage, but the light is so bright it fights its way through and flickers like Christmas lights on the crazy paving that meanders mysteriously around the garden. I can see only one piece of human intervention a simple sign stuck in the earth at the foot of a tree, a black metal plate about 30cm.x 10cm. with the word 'SILENCE' painted on it in white. Is this an unobtrusive instruction, an order, or a reminder to listen? The silence is disturbed by the tinkling of tea glasses as the lady returns with the customary glass of tea. We are offered a small delicate glass of amber tea complete with a chunk of sugar in a small china saucer. We gratefully sip our tea while the lady explains a little about the garden. In good English she tells us that she and her husband, Dr Mattar, are Palestinians and custodians of the tomb for a Christian charity based in London.

At the time of Jesus this garden belonged to one of the wealthiest men in the world, Joseph of Aramathaea. He was a very powerful man not just in Jerusalem but also throughout the Roman world. The garden was his sanctuary when attending the Jewish Sanhedrin and also very convenient for conducting business in the City. At the time of Jesus' crucifixion the tomb was new, in fact not quite complete and intended for Joseph himself. We accompany Mrs Mattar along the winding path for some fifty yards when we come to a rock cliff face. A small doorway has been cut for an entrance on which hangs an old wooden door. At the threshold and for several feet either side of the doorway is a gully about a foot wide, which has been cut into the stone floor. It is cut on a gradient and looks like it should carry storm water. This is the trough that the huge tomb boulder runs along. The picture books of childhood are misleading in depicting the tomb as being sealed with a large rock the shape of a cannon ball. In fact the stone is like a big stone cartwheel some six feet in diameter and about a foot thick. When in position it can roll down the slope and cover the opening, it would take four strong men with levers to roll it back along the gully. It is no wonder the biblical visitors to the tomb were surprised to find it re-opened on that first Easter Day. In addition to the sheer feat of strength there were also two official seals placed on the stone. The Roman seal issued by Pontius Pilate and the Jewish seal issued by Joseph, the breaking of either seal could result in the death penalty. On entering through the doorway I was expecting a small stone cell but we walk into a room, the size of a sitting room. It is almost square with ample headroom and completely empty. Then I notice as my eyes adjust to the dimness there is an extension going off to the left like a smaller room with a roughly cut coffin like recess in the floor. This is where two thousand years ago Jesus the Christ was laid to rest for two days and three nights. Mrs Matter says she will go and wait in the garden while we say a prayer.

I am stunned; I cannot say a prayer for bewilderment. Neither Lee or I could speak; we pace around looking at the blank walls. Then we notice a pale red cross painted on the wall with a small Alpha and Omega written alongside.

We walk out into the daylight to where Mrs Mattar is standing. She points out a hill across the way just visible through the trees, "That is Golgotha, the hill of the skull where Jesus died; if you look up at the cliff face you can see the eye holes, the nose and the teeth of a skull. When the sun shines from that direction you can see it clearly. At the bottom of the hill there is a pit, which you cannot see very well from the garden. That is where people used to be stoned to death including the martyr St. Stephen". Strolling back to the house I tell Mrs Mattar that I am confused. It is only two days ago that I had queued in single file with dozens of others to pass through the Holy Sepulchre deep in the heart of the Old City. It was like an underground cave, full of gold, silver and jewels, crowded with many believers of every Christian creed.

"Now you tell me that this secluded tomb in this tranquil garden is the real Holy Sepulchre."

She gives me a booklet and asks me to look at the evidence. I tell her my father has been a lay preacher for the Church of England all of his adult life and he knows nothing of this.

"How could he? You must tell him and he should come and see for himself. Meanwhile you can leave your bags here while you visit the City. If you have nowhere to stay you can stay here. If you are not afraid you can sleep the night in the tomb and I will arrange for a bed, but come back before dark because I do not open the gate after dark."

Lee and I looked at each other and then we nodded in agreement.

As Lee and I walk back silently into the Old City with its increasing bustle, I ask Lee what he makes of it all. He shrugs his shoulders and says,

"I am not a Christian believer, but I feel there is something in it but I cannot explain."

We both agree we can handle sleeping there, we will be dry and safe. Firstly, we need to eat and so find a street restaurant to eat our usual Shish Kebab and flat bread. After we have eaten we saunter through the bazaar and wind our way back to our new residence. On ringing the bell Mrs Mattar comes to the gate and escorts us along to the tomb. We now find there is a large mattress on the floor, two wooden chairs and a little table about three feet square. Our bags are parked against the wall behind the door. She smiles at us and looks pleased with herself. Lee looks perplexed and says,

"Why, err, how much is it a night?"

Mrs Mattar looks serious and says,

"There is no charge, this is not a hotel, and no price can be put on this. If it is your wish you can make a donation in the offering box by the house".

Mrs Mattar then goes on to explain that the garden is supported by voluntary contributions to the Garden Tomb Association, which was first set up by General Gordon in 1894. He was the man who first identified Golgotha by means of the bible and research while on one of his military stopovers in Jerusalem. General Gordon was convinced there must be a tomb in the vicinity of Golgotha. He raised money in England and excavated the area and so found this tomb, which has been buried here for nineteen hundred years. The Garden Tomb Association has maintained the garden ever since, its aims are to retain it in a natural state and to keep it tranquil as a place for contemplation and prayer and to avoid commercialism and superstition. Mrs Mattar wishes us a goodnight with a

"Sleep well".

We unroll our sleeping bags onto the mattress and fold our jumpers into pillows. I sleep heavily due to fatigue but I am disturbed by vivid dreams. Firstly, the horror of Roman crucifixion, the nailing and hanging on the cross and all that the execution entails and then the struggle of bringing the body from the hill above over the rough ground to lay it in the room where we are sleeping. My mind relived the traditional anointing and binding of the shroud and the rolling of the stone against the doorway. It was the solid bump of the stone locking me in that woke me up to find it was daybreak and all a dream.

Had it all been a dream? I scan the ceiling and walls and then crawl out of my sleeping bag. I put my jeans and jumper on and walk over to the chiselled out floor. I could visualise a body in a winding sheet and I wonder what is the truth. I need 'the loo' and make my way back through the garden to the toilet by the house, my foot just missing a bunch of grapes left on our doorstep by the kind lady. Mrs Mattar is a remarkable lady and she seems to have taken a liking to me. We have daily chats about the garden, religion and the sights to see in and around Jerusalem. Each evening on returning from our days adventures we find a present by the tomb door. Sometimes fruit, or a freshly baked cake and on one occasion a large cooked meal! Each day we would place our spare change into the offering box. We spend a lot of time in the City and we are getting to know the locals and they are getting to know us. I manage to get some part-time work with a sign writer and also spend a couple of hours each day sitting in a restaurant drawing portraits. The locals like it and they often tease each other over their likenesses. It was such a novelty for them that there was sometimes a queue and this casual work keeps me in food and pocket money. I even had one man bring his drawing back the following day to have his new hat added to it.

After a couple of weeks Lee and I meet two other lads, Mick, a huge American and Paul a lanky Englishman. They are also a travelling duo looking to spend Christmas in Jerusalem, which is now only a couple of weeks away. However, they cannot find any accommodation due to the influx of pilgrims and they spent last night in the Garden of Gethsemane. We would have liked to offer them refuge at the tomb but we thought Mrs Mattar would think we were taking advantage of her hospitality. Then the next day she tells us she is going to her sons in Beirut for Christmas and so the Garden will be closed for ten days while she and her husband are away. We are sorry to lose the tranquil paradise but it does stir us into action and we enquire about finding a room in the Old City. Apparently there is a family prepared to rent us a room some two hundred yards down from the Damascus Gate on the Via Dolorosa itself. We both go to view it and find a solid stone room with a domed ceiling three floors up. The stairways on these old properties are external with odd rooms off on different landings all owned or tenanted by different families. We then meet up with Mick and Paul and the four of us agree to rent the room, which has an attached washhouse and kitchen plus a communal toilet across the way. We have four beds, a table, four chairs and a primus stove. The 'water carrier' brings water in each day. The family of five move out immediately into a room on the next floor. Mick and Paul move in straight away and Lee and I follow after a further night at the Garden Tomb. In the morning we pack our things, I find I am collecting more and more possessions, far too many for me to carry. So I decide that the tent, which is heavy, is no longer useful in this climate. So I roll some spare clothes, a couple of books and tie them all up with a label marked 'To be collected' and place the bundle in a dark corner of the tomb. We thank Mrs Mattar profusely, wish her and her family a Happy Christmas and give an expectation to return in a few months. She takes back our gate key and waves us off down the road.

Chapter Six

Christmas in Jerusalem

We take our rucksacks straight to the new room and claim our beds. We celebrate our arrival by making tea on the primus in the kitchen. Well life is constantly changing and although we are now in the bustling Old City of Jerusalem, it is surprisingly quiet within the thick stonewalls of our room. Our day-to-day life goes on much the same apart from evenings, as there are now four of us. During the day I spend most of my time painting signs, drawing portraits and negotiating deals. I feel the need of a warm coat and I have seen some sheepskins being worked down the far end of the bazaar. The evenings are noticeably colder and I feel the need of an overcoat when out at night. The sheepskins here are very different from those back home, they are taken from the fat-tailed breed and the fleece hangs in ringlets more like hair than wool. The pelts are not fully tanned so there is a smell of stale sheep that hangs on the pelt. I have previously chatted to the tailor and on several occasions he has promised me a good price so now I will go and do a deal. We agree the jacket length plus cuffs and collar for a price of two pounds and one of my Swiss watches I bought in the Istanbul bazaar for one pound each. I had bought them to give as special gifts as I had been told that the modern look, Swiss label watches are highly sought in Arabia.

The next day I collect my bright white shaggy sheepskin jacket, which is thick and stiff. I feel very conspicuous in it and I no longer blend into the local scene so well as I did previously. When I first entered Syria I had purchased traditional Arab headdress in white plus a black cloak with gold trim. These and my dark complexion enable me to pass unnoticed almost anywhere in the Middle East. The Arab headdress I find to be a very convenient garment, it shields the head from the sun and yet it is easily draped around the face to protect from dust and can be dropped down around the shoulders like a loose scarf when indoors. I stride back to our room like an illuminated barrage balloon. When Mick sees it he says,

"Oh man I must have one of those", so the next day I take him to the tailors for a fitting.

Christmas is almost upon us and the processions passing our door along the Via Dolorosa are almost a daily occurrence. Christmas in Jerusalem lasts for several weeks because the different traditions have different dates for Christ's birthday. They spread from mid December to mid January, so by the time the Armenians, the Russian, Greek Orthodox, and Roman Catholics have all had their traditional ceremonies Christmas seems to have taken up permanent residence in our street. We four roommates have decided to stick to our customary December 25th and we have heard that on the night of the 24th there will be a carol service in the Shepherds Fields near Bethlehem. So that event is marked on our calendar a week before as an obligatory date for us all. The Old City is now bursting with visitors and the occupants of our room have swollen to a dozen. It seems that every time one of us goes out we tend to return with a lost soul from the English-speaking world who has nowhere to lay their head. Well, it is Christmas and even though we only have four beds we do have plenty of floor space. Each new arrival is vetted by the principal four and given an allocated space and a copy of the house rules. The rules are simple; assault, theft or any crime against the community is punishable by recompense and immediate eviction via the wall. The drop from the wall some two storeys up from the street below is about twenty feet and fortunately no one has ever been asked to leave via the wall. By the time there are fifteen of us living in the room the landlord becomes concerned at the increased occupation. Although he does not speak English it is clear from his waving of Dina notes that the rent has gone up. However, a quick whip round from the newcomers and he goes away smiling. Christmas is only two days away now and there are twenty-seven of us in the room. A rota is arranged for sleeping to ease the pressure. The principal four retain the right to sleep on the beds from midnight to 7am and at any time during the day a dozen people or more can be found asleep or resting. Each evening of our Christmas week we have a singsong of ballads and carols. We have two guitars, a banjo and enough folk singers to fill a church hall.

On the afternoon of Christmas Eve we all set off for Bethlehem, we board a bus at Damascus Gate and get off at Manger Square. Before the carol service we visit the Church of the Nativity, our motley crew are eyed with suspicion as we pass through the church under the constant gaze of the priests on duty. We file our way down the steps to the crypt where in an alcove of stone and marble a silver star about fifty centimetres across has been crafted into the floor, with incense burners hanging above. This marks the spot where the infant Jesus was born. We pay our tributes and each light a candle before re-emerging back into Manger Square.

It is almost dark and we are advised that the Shepherds Fields are a couple of miles away. So we set off on foot and I am really glad of my new warm coat. There is a cold wind and sleet in the air. A few of our company drop out of the trek and return to Jerusalem but most of us persevere and find our way to a gathering of about five hundred people on the hillside. There are a few lights, lanterns and a primitive sound system. I think there is an attempt by a choir somewhere in the middle but the sound is fluctuating erratically in the wind. We sing half a dozen carols before the cold and sleet drives us to re-trace our steps to Bethlehem. We feel it is something of a disappointment, a lot of effort for a poor spectacle and after walking hours in the cold we have worked up an appetite. By now there are a dozen of us left in search of a traditional Christmas dinner.

It's about nine o'clock on Christmas Eve and Bethlehem is dark, cold and deserted. We roam the streets looking for a restaurant and come upon a small deserted café about to close its doors. We are starving and cold and the poor owner looks horrified at the dishevelled band of foreigners, so he tries to say he is closed. Too late we are in and we agree with him that the café is now closed and we lock the door. We take off our wet clothes and re-arrange the small tables into one central table area and place the chairs around it. Now for Christmas dinner, how are we going to find suitable ingredients in this Arab kitchen? Mick, Barbara and I look through the kitchen and fridge to see what is available. We find five chickens, humus, tomatoes, beans, paprika and flat bread; a couple of melons and some oranges plus two and a half bottles of Arak (Arab Raki). Barbara thinks we can make a reasonable meal, so it is all put out on the kitchen worktable. I find a pencil and paper and indicate to the owner that we would like it all cooked up for the twelve of us and for him to write down his price. The poor man looks puzzled and retreats to the back kitchen returning a moment later with his wife. She looks non-too pleased at the arrival of their late and unexpected guests. All the gestures are looking negative while the two of them debate the issue. We three return to the table and sit with the others trying to look like good customers.

After what seems like an age but was probably more like five minutes the owner comes to the table with the paper and a price that amounts to ten pounds written on it. This is more than we expected but it does include the alcohol and with the unsocial hours we agree to the price and all put our share on a plate in the middle of the table. The sight of the money brings the kitchen to life and glasses of Arak are served to lighten the mood. Barbara hovers around the kitchen to make sure the chickens are well cooked and to supervise the plate presentation, ensuring it is in the English tradition rather than the Arabic. The café owners think it very odd that we all have a big plate with everything piled on. There is enough food for us all to have half a chicken with an assortment of cooked and fresh vegetables to be followed with a fresh fruit salad. Lee slips out to get another bottle of Arak and we continue our carol singing with Silent Night in German at which the café owner joins in. By the early hours we have eaten and drunk the café dry, we pay our ten pounds plus a collection of small change as a tip. It is agreed we can sleep the night in the café until the bus for Jerusalem arrives in the morning. This makes for a memorable Christmas with a difference.

On return to our room in Jerusalem Christmas has peaked. The only Christmas card I receive is from a friend of my mother's in the village back home, somehow that one got through and so has pride of place on the wall. Three days after Christmas our room is much depleted, most of the travellers have moved on. Crazy Paul is off to Kuwait to see how far it is. He has some goods, mainly silver jewellery bought cheaply in the bazaar and he believes it will fetch double the price in Kuwait. He suggests we give him five pounds for purchases and he will bring us ten pounds back. Several of us agree but Lee thinks it is a con, so Paul leaves for Kuwait and Lee leaves for Baghdad as he is tired of Jerusalem and wanting to move on. I agree to catch him up in the Spring. Mick, Barbara and I are now the only long standing residents left at the room.

I spend more and more time on my own and I sense I am becoming institutionalised. It is a big effort for me to go downstairs into the street and do a couple of hours drawing so that I can buy the meat, bread and fruit that make up my daily diet. Between drawings I sit in the teahouse watching the world go by- the poverty of the street urchins being driven off the Via Dolorosa by the well-heeled policeman trying to give an air of respectability for the benefit of the small groups of visitors doing the tourist route. Across the road from the teahouse is a carpet and metal-ware shop, which is always a hive of activity. Every shopkeeper has an errand boy sometimes only six or seven years old. They will fetch glasses of tea for customers or goods from other premises. This particular day I notice a young lad has brought the wrong carpet on a donkey for a waiting customer. The shopkeeper is furious, he shouts at the lad and clips him about the ears, the lad runs out crying, picking up a broomstick on his way, he hits the waiting donkey on the rump, the donkey startled, kicks out at a dog, which yelps and shoots off after a cat, which disappears down a side alley. In thirty seconds that sequence of events sums up what life is like for some out here.

One of the local police who I had seen pass by on many occasions stops to enquire about having his portrait drawn. I agree and he takes up his position on the seat in front of me. He is rather impatient and wants to see progress every few minutes; such behaviour is disturbing for me and usually makes for an inferior result. His desire to have as much of his uniform as possible showing calls for a fresh start but he will still have the half completed first drawing. The final drawing is not a good likeness but his uniform is well executed so he finds it acceptable. He proudly shows the people in the teahouse who dare not say anything other than agree with him and then he leaves to show his colleagues. I was half expecting to have a run of requests from the police station but not that day. He does come back later to say his friend the Mayor would like to see me and he will take me to meet him tomorrow.

He calls as arranged at the teahouse and we go along to a large stone building in the centre of the Old City. When we go inside I am surprised to be descending stairs to a large basement room where the Mayor is sitting at a table surrounded by about eight other men. I am introduced to them all in turn and then I am asked for my passport. It soon becomes clear that I have not been invited here to draw portraits. This is some sort of council meeting and my prolonged presence in the city has been noticed with some curiosity. My passport is scrutinised, with particular attention being given to countries I had previously visited. They seem reassured that I am English and not American and also that I have never visited Israel. The one gentleman at the side of the Mayor speaks good English and tries to keep me informed of the discussion. Some of the men are frowning and not convinced but the majority come to the conclusion that I am not an Israeli spy. There follows much debate without me being included after which the deputy acting as translator asks me if I would like to go to Israel. I tell them I have no plans to go and that I will be going east to Baghdad. I am aware that if I cross the wall into west Jerusalem I will not be permitted back into Jordan to continue my travels. When that is relayed back to the meeting it creates more debate. I am then given a lecture of how Israel is planning to take the old city and more of the west bank. The Palestinians have lost much land already and they have to be well prepared in order not to lose more. I sympathise and tell them I know people personally who have been waiting all their lives to return to their homes. The group looks expectantly at me as if they want to hear more. Then the mood changes and the translator asks me,

"Will you help us, we need to know where the big guns are and how many. If you will go we can get you across the border and back without your passport being stamped. We will give you a camera, map and information to cross and come back. We will give you a big reward for this". I am shocked; I do not know what to say. It is not to my liking but if I say no something may happen to me when I leave. If I say yes I become a spy and likely to be arrested or shot by the Israeli's. I must think fast and satisfy them immediately, though I know they are divided amongst themselves, so here goes,

"If I agree to do this it will not help you. Even if I get all the best information in one weeks time it will be out of date and a waste of time and money. It is not the big guns you need to be concerned about but their tanks. They can bring as many as they need at any time wherever they want. You need to be prepared for tanks; however, if you do find someone to do this work it will probably create an incident. This is just what the Israeli's are waiting for. They are looking for any excuse, any reason at all to advance into the Old City. Only two hundred yards and they are here. Something like this could give them the very reason that they want and then they will be in your city".

My words are relayed back to the meeting one sentence at a time; meanwhile there is total silence. Then they all start talking at once. The Mayor thumps the table and shakes his head. He thanks me and says I can go as they now have other business to talk about. The policeman escorts me out of the building and back into the street. I walk briskly back to the room wondering if I am being followed or if I have satisfied them. The next few days I spend much time meditating in the tranquil safety of the room, like a monk in his cell. Then one morning Mick says,

"Come on its time to take a trip."

He thinks we should take a trip to Akaba and the Red Sea. It is a straight road from Amman and we can probably get a lift in a truck straight through. So Mick, Barbara and myself pay a week's rent on the room, pack a light travel bag and take a bus to Amman.

Chapter Seven

The Rose Red City

Once in Amman we soon find the road to Akaba and we are picked up very quickly by a wagon destined for the port. Now these Arab wagons are something very different. They are huge high-sided metal crates with big cabs where you can sit five abreast. On top of the cab is a large metal roof rack where tarpaulins, tools and the driver's belongings tend to be stored. Up each side of the cab is a metal ladder welded on and the whole lorry is festooned with coloured lights, trophies and charms. The truck drivers seem to compete with each other to create the most colourful tableau. At night they look like illuminated stage sets gliding across the desert and can be seen from miles away. The drivers usually operate alone and their journeys can take many days, so they are keen to have company even if they cannot speak your language they will still chat and sing regardless.

The three of us get a ride in one of these huge trucks and we travel all day with just one tea stop at a stone and mud hut in the middle of nowhere, just a flat barren landscape in every direction for as far as you can see. The Arabian deserts vary in nature; they are not simply sand and dunes like you see in the films. There are great expanses of flat land, also rolling hills and small mountains in places. The desert we are crossing is mainly flat with rugged mountains in the south. The tarmac road disappears soon after leaving town and degenerates into a gravel track compacted by repeated wheels creating ruts and potholes. There are great expanses of black rocks that look like lumps of coal scattered everywhere. This was the old stomping ground of Lawrence of Arabia and pretty inhospitable it is. Occasionally you come across another truck or nomadic herdsman with their camels and sheep, but what they live on beats me.

When we reach Akaba it is somewhat disappointing. It is so small you would hardly call it a village, just a few stone houses and a store where we buy bread and dates. We walk down to the beach, which is at the top tip of the Red Sea and spend the night on the beach beside a quiet sea. As we lie there we can see the twinkling lights of Eilat across the water in Israel. Chatting late into the night we swap stories of our travels and folks back home. Barbara tops the bill by telling us she is the niece of the Australian Prime Minister. She showed us a letter with the Australian Government heading and his signature giving her freedom of passage and personal assistance with a private phone number to call in emergencies. Barbara is a typical travelling Aussie and I cannot see her ever needing to use it, unless of course war with Israel was declared overnight.

The next day we swim in the Red Sea and sunbathe on the beach. Even though it is winter, during the day it is hotter than summer in England. After we have soaked up the sun we stroll back into town to look for a meal. The only restaurant we can find has just one table in one room, so when we sit down we fill it. It is the custom to look at the range of food on offer and pick your choice. I stick with chicken and chickpeas, Mick thinks he will have egg, beans and peppers. The eggs are smaller than we are used to so he picks three out of the tray and hands them over for the pan. When the cook breaks the second egg a half developed chick pops out, which he discards and points to the egg box. Mick looks horrified and hesitant, and then the cook comes round takes a couple of the eggs and Mick by the arm to the door. The cook then shakes the egg against his ear and holds it up against the sun. He is looking and listening to see if there is a chick inside each egg! That's enough of chicken roulette for Mick, the eggs go back in the box and he changes his mind and chooses a full size chicken like Barbara and me.

After eating we stroll back out on the road for Amman. On the outskirts of the town there is a Bedouin encampment with camels and horses tethered around their tents. Some of the men are curious and walk over to meet us. We shake hands and are invited to take tea in their tent. Although we cannot converse we manage to get by with sign language. They want to show us their animals (their wealth) and they have some beautiful Arab horses. One of them saddles up a grey stallion and invites Mick and myself to have a ride. We both decline but our Barbara steps forward, which takes them and us by surprise. Barbara happens to be an equestrian superwoman; she circles the compound twice and then shoots off across the desert in a cloud of dust. By now all the family have come out and are staring unbelievably across the desert amid chatter and excitement. It is about ten minutes later when the cloud of dust returns and Barbara dismounts the high stepping snorting stallion saying,

"Not a bad mount."

She is a local hero and the Arak comes out, with cheers and hand shakes all round.

Following the Barbara celebrations we make our way north on foot until we are offered a lift in a sheep wagon. The driver has obviously seen or heard about Barbara's feat as he keeps looking at her and making horse riding gestures, which she finds a bit much after half an hour. After a couple of hours the driver stops and indicates that he is turning off the main track and going to Petra. We had all heard of Petra, the Rose Red City of Antiquity and so we agreed we would go with him. Why not, as we are so close it would be a shame to miss it. I recollect that it had been rediscovered some years earlier after being lost for centuries. It used to be a prominent city on the trade route two thousand years ago bringing silks and spices from the Far East. I believe trade collapsed after the fall of the Roman Empire and the City then became deserted and lost. We parted company with our driver when he dropped us at a footpath by a small battered metal sign saying Petra. There is nothing here, nothing to see, just barren desert apart from a narrow path disappearing down into a ravine. We follow it for half an hour descending lower and lower with a cliff face rising higher and higher either side of us. The ground is rough and in places the passage through the rocks is only just wide enough for two people to walk side by side. Then suddenly the path begins to widen and huge relief carvings appear on the walls of the cliff. Doorways and windows of a huge dimension are carved in the red sandstone. As we explore them it appears they have little depth, just one room or two at the most leading off each doorway. The path now widens rapidly to reveal a huge basin with cliffs all around and then a flat floor a mile or more across like a huge oval bathtub. The floor has some paved streets with remnants of stone pillars in columns, some are twenty feet tall but most are broken down and are just a few feet high. This had once been a magnificent city but now there is little left but the remnants of a stone shell.

I can now understand how Petra was lost for centuries because up on the desert level there is nothing to see. From up there it just looks like continuous desert, you would not see the city until you were about to walk off the cliff. Looking around I wonder how one reaches the buildings on the upper levels of the cliff face. Perhaps originally there were stone or wooden stairways attached to the cliff in order to give access to the upper levels but there is nothing there now. We walk right across the arena to the far side where we notice one of the ground floor stone rooms is a shop of sorts. An elderly man sits on a stool by the door and inside is a table and some boxes with unrecognisable things inside. The only things I can recognise are tobacco leaves hanging from the ceiling and a barrel of loose dates in front of the table. The shopkeeper sits motionless just giving us a

"Salaam Ali koom", he probably realises he has nothing that we would be interested in. The whole city looks deserted with no sign of habitation other than this old man in his cave, which would have looked poverty-stricken two thousand years ago. The sun is coming down now and Barbara is concerned about getting back to the road before dark. I am very tired and need to rest and I have doubts that there is time to make the road before dark. Also I wanted to spend more time exploring the city and hopefully to do some drawings. We all agree to meet back at the room in Jerusalem, so Mick and Barbara set off back for Amman and I climb to one of the higher levels to look for somewhere to spend the night.

I manage to find what is little more than a cave in the rock face up quite a steep and difficult climb. I sit on the doorstep to have my supper of bread and dates and watch a glorious sunset, which really brings out

Mad Dogs and an Englishman

the red of the Rose Red City. Whenever travelling for more than a day I would carry emergency rations, which usually comprise of a couple of sheets of flat bread, a pack of dates, a packet of Feta cheese, a plastic pot of honey and naturally a bottle of water. I know that when there is only half a sun left above the horizon it will be pitch black in a few minutes. So I withdraw to the back of the cave, roll out my sleeping bag as a mattress, fold my jumper for a pillow and put my warm sheepskin coat back on. I am a little concerned about wild dogs coming in search of a meal, so I attach a flare onto my pistol just in case. I know the flare will frighten any wild animal and while in the cave a gas cartridge is just as likely to affect me as any attacker. So I settle down to sleep with my pistol under my pillow.

I sleep heavily for a while and then I awake suddenly for no apparent reason. When you are travelling you learn to sleep in all sorts of situations and places, still sleeping well but with a heightened awareness. Anything out of the ordinary, the slightest noise and I awake to a state of full awareness. I lie motionless listening for a cue. I hear a rustle, a movement by my rucksack only a few feet away but I can see nothing at all, I reach for my pistol and slip off the safety catch, I am listening for panting for breathing or the next movement from by my rucksack but there is just silence. I feel a presence; I am suspecting a wild dog has scented my food. Then I hear a buckle jingle on my rucksack flap. Definitely there is something at my rucksack and thoughts start rushing through my head. Do I jump up and shout or just fire the gun in that direction? I decide to jump up and shout, so I slowly move my feet and lever myself onto one knee when I feel a rapid tug on my left sleeve, I shout loudly as I feel my sleeve being pulled, I think it is a dog's jaw and while I am still thinking I pull the trigger while pointing the gun in the direction of the tug. The whole cave lights up with an orange glow; there is a man not three feet away and a knife shining in his hand and a red check headdress wound around his head. The flare burns furiously between us but unfortunately for him it attaches to his robes. I was shouting and screaming; he gave a high-pitched continuous scream as he turned, running for the entrance surrounded by an incandescent orange glow trailing pungent smoke. I follow him to the entrance keeping a distance of some twenty feet. He runs jumping and leaping down the rugged approach. The flare gives him good sight of the boulders and obstacles for about some fifty metres before it falls off his clothes. He disappears to the left and I see him fleeing across the basin floor as the fallen flare weakens and then fizzles out. It is the nearest thing to a human firework I have ever seen. I am shaking, trembling with fright and my heart pounding in my chest so much I could hear it as well as feel it. I have to get out of the cave, he might return with others and if anything happens to me I would never ever be found in such an isolated place. I look at my watch, the one my Gran gave me for my twenty-first birthday with an illuminated dial. It is four thirty and several hours before dawn. I pack my rucksack, attach another flare on my pistol, put the safety catch on and replace it in the holster on my belt. I put my pack on my back and very cautiously pick my way down the rugged slope.

    I remember thinking earlier while eating my supper that I would have to stay until daybreak, as there was no way I could safely climb down in the dark without the risk of breaking a leg. Either way, stay or go there is little to choose. I pause as my eyes adjust to the night sky. I can make out the big boulders and the steep drops. I could slide some of the way on my bottom using my pack like a sledge. I take my time descending over the rough ground and then make up for lost time when I reach the flat. I make off to the right in the opposite direction from the attacker and head for the old paved highway in order to cross the basin directly and reach the ravine entrance. It is about a mile and a half before I reach the ravine where it is still too dark to climb safely. I feel I have put good distance between my attacker and me so I choose a rocky ledge to sit on that gives me a clear view across the basin. Here I will wait for enough light to enable me to pick my way through the ravine and back onto the main road. I ponder on my lucky escape and keep a careful watch for movement or lights approaching across the empty arena.

    At the approach of dawn I tentatively pick my way back up the ravine for about a mile or so before reaching the flat of the desert and the dusty track of the Akaba road. I sit at the side of the track hoping that a truck will come soon before anyone can follow me. I have a clear view for several miles in both directions on the road and there is nothing but flat, rough ground. After about an hour of undisturbed silence I notice a ball of dust coming from the direction of Akaba. The sun is climbing into the sky, and feeling warm I take some water from my bottle and wait with anticipation for the truck to reach me. It is a large, long distance wagon loaded with what looks like bananas. The driver slows to a standstill and beckons me to get in. I call

"Amman"?

He nods with his eyes followed by the usual greeting. He speaks no English but I am so relieved to be heading back to civilisation. My mind jumps from what has happened to the thoughts of my attacker. How did he know where I was? He must have watched me climb up to the cave or maybe the shopkeeper had told him? Then I wondered how many times El Lawrence had travelled up and down this roadway. I woke up with a start when the engine switched off and instinctively felt for my gun. Was it happening all over again or was it just a dream. The driver looked curiously at me and shouted

"Chay". A welcome tea stop; I sip my tea and examine my sleeve where there is a cut about four inches long at the elbow in my nice new coat. Fortunately the blade had somehow completely missed my arm, the sleeve is so thick and my arm so thin. The tear is the only physical reminder I have that it has not all been a bad dream.

Next day I am back in the safety of the room in Jerusalem relating my horror story to Barbara and Mick. Barbara kept saying,

"You should have come back with us."and Mick said,

"Man you are lucky". I feel lucky, relieved but exhausted. Mentally and physically flat, but appreciative that I am still alive and uninjured. Night and day I am sleeping heavily and having vivid dreams about all manner of things from Christmas dinners to drowning in sea and sand.

The next day Paul returns from his trip to Kuwait. We could not believe he had done the round trip in only seven days. He gave me ten pounds in Kuwaiti dinars; double my investment, which is a lot of money to me. I offered him a couple of pounds but he refused saying,

"No, that was the deal".

My spirits were raised somewhat and I saw the crazy man in a new light. The Paul that was forever messing about and acting the fool has a core of cool steel. Not only is he streetwise to the extreme, he is dead honest and reliable. The times I've heard people say, "You won't see that madman again." In the back of my mind I had thought them probably right, not that I thought he would intentionally 'do a runner,' but that the odds of his success were small. Within a couple of days I have slipped back into the melancholic atmosphere of the room accomplishing little apart from getting the coat man to repair the knife cut in my sleeve. He just laughed at my tale and to my surprise he sewed a diamond shape patch over the gash. I wear it like a war trophy and ponder on the fate of the attacker, not that I will consider returning to Petra to find out. Mick and Barbara decide to move on to Damascus and so I am the only one left at the room with little appetite for anything apart from a good meal, which is difficult to find in my circumstances. The rent of the room now falls totally on me and the cost will be too much for me to sustain for long.

I go to collect post from the Consulate and find a letter from home telling me, yet again, to be careful and that the old man next door has died. There is also a surprise letter from Lee saying he is having a great time in Baghdad and giving me an address where he is waiting for me to join him. Well that is the kick-start I need, so I go and have a good meal, a full nights sleep and then pay off the rent on the room. The landlord looks disappointed at the news of my departure but I know in my heart that the time to move on has come. The excitement of Christmas and Petra has passed and the open road is awaiting me yet again.

Chapter Eight

Deep in the Desert

I take the local bus from the Damascus Gate to the capital Amman. I always seem to be passing through Amman rather than looking round it. Here I am again on the road east, this time for Baghdad. Almost straight away I catch one of these large desert trucks covered in fairy lights. The driver is a dark skinned Arab in his thirties who speaks no English but understands the word Baghdad. He keeps looking at me and grinning and I am wishing he would keep his eyes on the road, which is full of ruts, potholes and boulders. We have a few hundred miles of nothingness now, just wilderness with the occasional group of nomads and the odd truck. It is very bumpy, dusty and warm. Mid winter in the desert is very hot in the day and very cold at night. Hour after hour pass by with no sign of habitation. I try to pass the time by dozing but with the roar of the engine and the continual bumps it is very difficult. I count the big bumps, one very big one to nine or ten smaller ones. If it gets to one in four the road is very bad and I need to hold on with both hands. The lorry drivers in Europe do not know they are born.

Departing from my story for a moment, I would like to tell the reader of another traveller who came this way one hundred and thirty years previously. In 1835 a wealthy young man in his early twenties took a similar route across Europe through Turkey to Palestine to

Michael Benton

become lost in the very same desert I am about to cross. Some years after my trek I read about Alexander Kinglake and his "Grand Tour" in his book "Eothen" (From the East). Following his classical education at Eton and Cambridge he travelled on horseback with servants and a baggage train containing his requirements to cross what was then the Ottoman Empire. After repeated rejections by publishers, his book was eventually printed in 1844 at his own expense. It became an overnight best seller and one of the publishers who rejected his manuscript then considered it was the greatest business error of his life. Anyone reading that masterpiece will not only be struck by the similarities of our adventures but also the marked differences that have occurred in the one hundred and thirty year interval. Throughout my writing I am tempted to quote from his work but the comparison would put my writing in such a poor light I would probably have given up by this point.

Kinglake was bemused that the Arab mind could not understand by what privilege an Englishman with just a pistol could travel the desert alone, whereas the locals were obliged to travel in much larger numbers to ensure their safety. He was even asked if he did it by magic and how much he would want to reveal his secret. Kinglake does give an explanation for the secret in his book and it appears to be mainly an English attribute found in abundance in his character and to lesser extent in mine. It has also been amusingly noted that mad dogs also possess this peculiar ability in hot and arid places.

During the day we make a couple of truck stops at tea huts in the middle of nowhere for snacks of goat's meat and tea. About an hour after dark the driver pulls up for the night and we prepare to bed down. The driver has a single bunk in the space behind the seats. He beckons me to join him in the bunk but I decline and wrap my sleeping bag around me and stretch out across the front seats. After an hour or so of sleep a hand groping my bottom disturbs me. With a jolt I hit out, the driver recoils and mutters in Arabic. There are two more attempts and a struggle for a couple of minutes before I call it a day, open the door and climb out of the cab. There is a light wind and the air is cold. I think my best bet is to climb up onto the storage rack above the cab to be well clear of any predators. So I haul my rucksack and sleeping bag up the metal ladder onto the top. I feel my hands sticking to the rungs

Mad Dogs and an Englishman

as I climb and by the third rung I realise the metal is so cold the frost is pulling the skin off my hands when I release my grip. I pull my jumper sleeves down over my hands for protection and climb up into the metal cradle. There is allsorts of junk up here but I wrap my sleeping bag around me and then pull a tarpaulin completely over the top of me. It is so stiff with the frost I have to kick it to make it bend and fold around me. Eventually I settle and manage to get some sleep before the rising sun wakes me. I lie quietly waiting until I can hear noises below and then climb down the ladder to face a very disgruntled driver. He makes it clear with abrupt words and gestures that he is not taking me any further. I am to stay put and wait for another lorry. He then climbs into his lorry and drives off leaving me standing there alone and completely isolated. Now what! There is no point in walking; I would only use up vital energy getting nowhere. I know I am approximately on a truck route but there are no kerbs or signs to say this is a road. The drivers just follow the tracks of other vehicles and so the road can be two or three miles wide.

The sun rises fast in the early morning and the heat becomes unbearable within an hour or so. I decide I need a shelter or shade at least and quickly. I find a depression in the ground and then collect rocks to build a semi-circular wall around it. Just a few feet across will be enough to give me protection from the wind and if I can build it about two or three feet high I can spread my sleeping bag across the top for shade. It takes me most of the morning to build this primitive semi-circular igloo and it is just big enough for me to sit inside. While collecting the rocks I come across the jawbone of a sheep or a goat and it brings to mind the story of Samson that I heard years ago in Sunday School. When the Philistines set upon Samson he just happened to find the jawbone of an Ass with which to slay them. How ridiculous I thought. As if he would just find the jawbone of an ass like that lying conveniently on the ground. Well out here you do, even in the desert one finds jaw bones, skulls and leg bones of sheep, camels and asses just lying around, bleached by the sun they stand out and appear unexpectedly even in the most unusual places.

Now it is so hot even under cover I wonder whether all my efforts have been worth it. Then of course there is a possibility of a sandstorm and the shelter will be essential for that. The wind is a phenomenon to be avoided if at all possible. A light wind may feel like a refreshing breeze until the point that it lifts the loose sand from the desert floor. Then you can see clouds of dust rolling across the desert and at this time one can get dust in the eyes, which is very irritating and annoying that protective action had not been taken earlier. Out in the open the only protection is to wrap ones Kaffayer (headdress) around the face and tuck it in the headband. If one does not take cover, the increasing wind will drive the sand, which on hitting exposed flesh comes like the sting of an insect bite. Multiply that by a thousand times a second and your skin can be scraped raw in a few minutes just as if it has been enthusiastically sandpapered. It was my luck to experience a brief sand storm whilst sheltering in the stone hut, even though the wall reduces the force by ninety percent the dust still swirls around inside. I crouch into a ball and am completely covered up; I wait for an hour or so throughout the fury before the wind drops and calm returns. I find my clothes full of sand; each fold and crevice has a hand full of the stuff. My face has a film all over where it has stuck to my sweat. It is caked in my mouth, nostrils, eyes and ears. My scalp is like a field with a crop of hair pushing through. Days later I am still scraping sand out of my ears and scalp with my fingernails. However, I feel lucky that it was not more ferocious and of a longer duration.

Water is a scarcity out here, particularly in the desert and my one and a half bottles is only enough for a day but with care maybe I can spin it out to last two days. Hopefully in that time I will find a lorry but so far after half a day I see and hear nothing. My mind drifts as I sit in my stone hut pondering on how I got myself into this situation. It had never occurred to me that sexual favours would be expected of me in lieu of a lorry ride. Lady travellers are well aware of the rigours and risks of such adventures and that is why so many of them team up with a trusted chap. However, I am learning that anything can happen to anyone in this strange world between East and West. I think of Lee somewhere in Baghdad waiting for me and wonder how long he will wait before he gives up and moves on to Pakistan. I think of my mom and dad and folks back home, I know some think me mad, and others who told me I was foolish for coming penniless into the wild east. Will I return safely to my roots or be lost in the desert never to be heard of again? Then I see a cloud of dust on the horizon, it is surely a lorry

Mad Dogs and an Englishman

but I soon realise it is moving across my line of vision not towards me, about a mile away. I can only just see the lorry at the front of the dust trail and within a few minutes he has gone and then his dust trail fades into the atmosphere.

The sun is overhead now and very hot, what a good job I have got my little shelter. Sweat forms on my head and runs down the back of my neck, down my forehead, around and into my eyes, stinging due to the high salt content. I thought eyebrows where supposed to keep sweat out of your eyes but apparently not here. Skin sticks to skin and muscles burn with an internal fire. My mouth and throat are dry and feel like they are full of concrete dust, my lips stick together and little shreds of skin pull off when I open my mouth to moisten my lips with my tongue. My head aches and I see flashes like fork lightning hitting my eyelids when I close my eyes. My burning eyes seem to be as big as tennis balls and my ears hum and sing. The old music hall song "Only mad dogs and Englishmen go out in the mid-day sun" repeatedly echoes in my head, but here is one Englishman who would willingly opt out. In the fierce heat I hear distant church bells, which logically cannot be there. Maybe it is the bell of a leading goat but most probably it is all in my head, it is very difficult to tell what is real and what is imagined.

It is strange how big the sun seems in the desert sky, the barren landscape stretches to infinity in every direction and the sun dominates everything. It seems especially large when it is on or near the horizon, so big it is unreal. It is dipping into the horizon now and I can expect an hour of comfortable temperature before the intense cold creeps in. I need to take my sleeping bag off the roof in readiness to wrap around me. I put on extra socks and my spare jumper, put my boots back on and wrap both my headscarves around my head. I load my revolver with blank and gas cartridges and screw the flare attachment on the barrel. I place the gun and the flares on a flat stone by my side. I do not expect any human intrusion but I am aware there are wild desert dogs that hole up during the day and come out hunting at night. Hopefully they will stay in the vicinity of Bedouin encampments and not come sniffing out my meagre rations. The night seems endless, I hear the irregular yaps of the desert dogs and I only manage a few snatches of sleep. The silence seems more intense at night and I also hear noises in my ears, which I have never noticed before. I see shapes moving in the darkness, which I know cannot really be there. The night sky is so clear and there is a deep blue about its blackness. The stars are so much brighter and more numerous, maybe the atmosphere is clearer and you can see further into space. The moon also looks bigger than usual, but not as overwhelming as the sun. My extremities start to feel the cold first with tingling and loss of use in fingers and toes. I shiver and ache in all my joints. The cold air hits like cold steel, high up my nose between my eyes. I automatically pull myself into a ball with my hands tucked under my sheepskin jacket. I would die now without my jacket and I do not know which is worse the heat of the day or the cold of the night.

Eventually dawn arrives bringing a huge orange sun pushing up out of the horizon, throwing fierce light from one end of my world to the other. It is time to stretch my legs but they are reluctant to move, particularly my knees. I think I ought to go to the toilet, as it is several days since I had a bowel movement and a day or so since I passed water. However, if you do not put it in it cannot come out. My bottled water is almost gone, just about a cupful left that I use simply to moisten my lips. I must get a lift today or else I am in serious trouble. I know I am suffering from dehydration and malnutrition but I know I can resolve that when I return to civilisation. Then I notice my abdomen is distended, suddenly overnight I have a balloon belly that is becoming more uncomfortable by the hour. I return my sleeping bag to the roof and crawl back inside. Perhaps I ought to fly my flag off the roof, not that there is anyone to see it, but maybe if I am not rescued, some time in the future my remains can be returned to the British Embassy. I unpin the flag from my rucksack and tie it on a piece of thorn twig that I push into the stones on top of the structure. I manage to get a little comfortable sleep for a couple of hours before the heat of the day wakes me. I stand up to scan the desert for any sign of movement but there is nothing anywhere. This is the very desert that T.E. Lawrence struggled in fifty years ago through great adversity. In his Seven Pillars of Wisdom he describes the country, people and customs. His horrific torture and sexual abuse carried out by his Turkish captors makes my experience seem like a tea party. El Lawrence is still a legend in these parts.

Constantly I see mirages, the desert floor will not keep still, my wobbly eyes and the heat haze play tricks on me. If there really were something there I probably would not believe it. I need to stretch out to ease my belly, which puts my legs in the full sun. I ease one problem and it creates another, I know I am at a low ebb, the lowest I have ever been but I am not afraid. There is a strange peace around me and within me. An acceptance of what will be will be. Still I have hope of being found, though it is not the end of the world if I am not. Just the end of my little world. The day burns on and I am losing the ability to think straight. One moment I am lying on a beach in Greece waiting for the drinks man and he is being a very long time. Then I am back home walking on the common and mother will be wondering where I am. Oh yes, mother will be wondering where I am. I drift in and out of sleep or something similar.

It is at this point I experience a strange type of out of body experience. I expect it is triggered by my low state and my concern for my anxious mother back home. I am sitting crouched in my little shelter when I leave my body in the form of a wisp of white light through the top of my head vertically into the sky. I travel like a shooting star in an arc across Arabia and Europe. In the space of a few seconds I land on ephemeral feet springing lightly onto the grass slopes of the common just five hundred yards from my home in England. I walk lightly and briskly along the road in the time frame it would normally take and then enter my family home by the back door. My mother and father are going about their evening chores. I talk to them but they do not hear me. I can see them but they do not appear to see me. I hold my mother to me and say, "I am safe it is all okay", but she cannot see, hear or feel me. She tells my father that she thinks I am in trouble and she is worried that I need help, but neither they nor anybody else knows where I am. My father reassures her in his usual calm and concise way that I am okay otherwise they would have heard. I realise I cannot get through to them and withdraw. Strangely I retrace my steps walking backwards to the point where I landed on the common. I then shoot off in a reverse arc across the sky to descend back through the top of my head. I am still unmoved in my little hut.

The next thing I know is that the sun is down again and another cold night approaches. I have heard that it is less painful to die from the cold than the heat but for me there seems little to choose between them. I have lost my energy and motivation to do anything about anything. I have enjoyed my life; there could have been more of it, but when your time is up, it's up. It is at this point I lose track of events and all sensible thought.

Hot days and cold nights do not seem so extreme. Now a shadow of a figure appears just in front of me. At first I think it is the robber from Petra, or is it the Angel of Death? He moves slowly into my face and my ears hear,

"Salaam Ali koom", the Arabic greeting of peace.

I wonder, do angels speak Arabic?

"Ali koom salaam" I mutter and the vision disappears.

I must be hallucinating; there is nothing there now. Then suddenly the face reappears and pushes a goatskin water bottle between my lips. Ah thank goodness. Water! and plenty of it. Now I am aware of several others about me and being moved and carried but where and on what I do not know, but I think I am on a horse sitting behind a rider.

My next awareness is within a Bedouin tent being given a bowl of yoghurt. I am surrounded by women and children all busy with my welfare. I complain of my belly and watch while one woman walks out into the desert directly in front of me. She stoops a few times and returns with some dirty and dusty leaves, which she puts in a cooking pot with water and brews it like tea. Within a few minutes of drinking the brew I feel a calming effect on my abdominal cramps. I am lying on a bed made up of hard packed carpets; they are rough and hairy. The cooking pot is just a few feet away being tended by a couple of women. There are six or seven children of different ages who come near me to peer and giggle but as time goes on they lose interest and leave me to my slumbers. I feel safe yet unconcerned as to my whereabouts or my future. Sleeping and eating is all I do and the passing of time goes by unchecked.

After a couple of days or maybe three, a truck loaded with sheep pulls up outside the tent. I am assisted to my feet and pushed up into the cab. The family wave and cheer as I am driven away, but to where I have no idea and I do not particularly care. A days drive across the bumpy desert and I see a town coming into sight. A sign at the side of the road says Amman. Well I am back here yet again. The driver goes into the centre and through the gates of a building labelled The American Hospital. I bet they have never seen an ambulance like this before. The driver helps me down from the cab and hands me over to a nurse dressed like a nun. I give them my passport and they give me a bed. Within an hour a doctor has examined me and my belly. The nurse gives me some tablets and sets up a drip; I cannot believe how quickly I start to feel better. Within hours my head is clearing. I can see and hear properly once more. They give me regular meals of good food and in three days I feel a new man. The doctor says I can be discharged and I am free to go. He explains to me that there is no charge that the hospital is a charity and is staffed by an order of nuns. I am told if I wish I can make a donation and as I am very grateful for their assistance I give them half the cash I have on me. I leave with a spring in my step to try again on the road for Baghdad.

I feel very different after my experience in the desert. I am now completely fearless in all situations; I can take whatever life throws at me. I am not afraid of dying and I have an inner peace and calm that I cannot put into words. This feeling is to remain with me for many years. It would be a very long time before I was to experience caution and suspicion that most people would take for granted. If there is one thing in my life I should be grateful for it is that near death experience at being abandoned in total isolation in the hostile environment of the desert. There is no doubt it has had a profound influence on how I live my life.

Chapter Nine

Iraq and Iran

The road to Baghdad beckons and I wonder if Lee is still waiting for me. I hitch another big truck, which follows in the same tracks as two weeks previously. Hopefully this driver will behave himself and not give me any hassle. Fortunately he seems to be a good man and he lets me sleep unmolested in the cab overnight. At the end of the second day we reach the capital, a big city but rather boring. There are a few modern shops and a monument or two in the centre surrounded by a large urban sprawl. I make my way to the address given by Lee but alas he has moved on about a week before. That's the way it is on the road. However, I can rent his old room while I look around and work out my next move. A couple of days in Baghdad and I have seen the mosque, the museum, the shops and the bazaar. I feel a little disappointed, as Lee had made it sound so good, perhaps I am missing something somewhere. Anyway I move on and head for Tehran, the capital of mystic Persia, the land of flying carpets, and now renamed Iran. Another bumpy truck journey, this time with a Christian Armenian who speaks a little English. He is a very kind and courteous man who insists on paying for my drinks and meals on route.

As we travel the ground rises and the air becomes cooler. Tehran has more splendour than Baghdad and I find it rather impressive in comparison. The people are kind and helpful and when I ask a policeman for directions he takes me into a teashop and buys me a drink! He speaks a little English and is obviously wishing to practice it. He tries to tell me about his city, which he is obviously very proud of. After we have finished our drinks he says he would like to take me to his home to meet his wife, which I accept. We arrive at a modern apartment at mealtime and I am invited to sit on a carpeted floor with various dishes of unknown contents placed on a large white cloth placed on the floor between us. It is an enjoyable meal and as I can pick and choose the things I like the taste of, the time passes quickly. Following an hour or so of conversation I am persuaded to stay the night and given a carpeted bunk in a room on my own. A policeman in Iran appears to have prestige and money, and there is no shortage of the necessities in his well furnished home. When I walk with him in the street people give way to him and are cautious in deed and speech. When he sees my pistol he is curious to examine it and seems to consider it a toy compared to his, which of course it is. He takes his pistol out of its holster empties the bullets into his hand and then gives it to me to examine while he tries to explain how it works. The next morning we rise to a breakfast of yoghurt and biscuits. Then he gives me a map of the city on which he has marked some places of interest that he thinks I should see. As he leaves for work he suggests I leave my rucksack in his house and return tonight to tell him what I have seen during the day. Ali leaves for duty and I set off on my tour of the city.

I find a large decorative mosque with lots of men about their ablutions at the taps and pedestals in the courtyard. Within the huge carpeted dome the walls are completely tiled in turquoise, blue and gold with abstract motives of flowers, quite impressive, almost comparable to the blue mosque in Istanbul but not as big. I find a museum and wander around looking at Iran's history before buying a meat filled pancake from a street vendor for lunch. I continue to stroll around the centre viewing the modern shops and buildings, when unexpectedly I come across the Shah's Golestan Palace where armed soldiers are positioned strategically around the gardens and one either side of the front door. I walk freely around the gardens and rest on a stone bench while I consider whether to try gaining access into the Palace. I notice that no one else comes into the garden area; the locals walk around and do not attempt to take short cuts through the gardens. Oh well,

I will give it a try, I will walk straight up the main path and through the front door and the guards will just block my path if they wish to. I do just that and the guards do not move. I walk confidently on holding my breath and waiting for a shout from the guards but there is nothing except the sound of my footsteps on the marble floor. Maybe my clean white headdress instead of my usual red chequered one acted as a passport. I wander through the deserted corridors and various rooms sparsely but lavishly furnished until I come to an enormous State Room. It is rather dark, and hanging from the ceiling are a series of large illuminated chandeliers, dazzling to look at but not giving off much reflective light.

Then I notice against the long wall what looks like a throne on a large dais. Yes, this must be the famous Peacock Throne. I must try to get a photograph of it but I only have my cine camera with me and the light is very poor so I doubt it will come out. It is indeed beautiful and quietly I climb up onto the dais and cheekily sit down on the throne to a completely empty auditorium. I dismount the throne, cross the room and find a staircase which I start to climb, however, at the top I feel that I am intruding into private apartments rather than viewing State Rooms. That would be over stepping the mark if I have not done so already. So I retrace my steps without coming across a single person and come out of the front door into the bright sunlit gardens, once again walking through the courtyard to the main street without being challenged. I could not believe what I had just done and seen, and later when I tell Ali the policeman he looks at me in disbelief and then thinks his English is letting him down. I find it difficult to believe myself but I have the film to prove it.

Another night with Ali and his wife is spent talking about his job and the political situation. He tells me that at this time the Shah is in America and there are concerns about his health and what might happen if he dies. There is definitely unrest in the air but Ali is unable to explain the details to me. I think I have stayed with Ali long enough and feel I should move on, however, the road east and north is mountainous and still blocked. I look at my map and decide to move to a warmer climate until summer arrives. Kuwait looks like a safe haven and a fairly straightforward road. So I take the road south with a series of small vehicles and my next main stop is Isfahan.

Isfahan is a very old and architecturally beautiful city. I spend hours wandering the streets and buildings marvelling at the ornate structures and colourful tiles. While I am resting in a courtyard of a mosque, a young man who looks a little older than myself approaches me. He speaks reasonably good English and explains that he is a student and he would very much like to show me his mosque. I accompany him firstly around the outside where he explains the washing procedures at the taps and the minimum requirements expected of a good Muslim. Then we go inside leaving our shoes at the door. Walking on several layers of carpets he shows where the Imam stands, where the men pray and the smaller ladies gallery. It looks like religion here is predominantly a man's thing, well in the public arena at least. We kneel together on the thick carpets and he demonstrates a prayer routine complete with prostrations, though I am lost with the words, he rattles them off as though I understand Arabic.

My newfound friend Abdullah invites me back to his room. It appears he is a student of Islam and he is resident in the mosque. His room is an old cell about ten feet square, one of a number in a row around the main building. It has a door, a small shuttered window, a bed, table, chair and a few books. Very austere and as plain and simple as it could possibly be in complete contrast to the elaborate decoration of the mosque. Abdullah is very enthusiastic about Islam and appears to want to impart all his knowledge to me today. He tries translating from the Koran but he has difficulty. Either the scripture is too profound or his English inadequate for the subject, or possibly both. He tells me something of Islam's Sharia Law. The loss of a hand for theft, stoning for adultery and hanging for certain other crimes. It all sounds rather barbaric and simplistic to me. However, this is his country and culture and I must respect it. At least the people know what to expect if they break their laws, but I do not think for a moment such ways would ever be tolerated in Britain. We then take a break and go for a walk buying a snack from a street vendor and a bottle of water to take back to his room.

On returning he resumes his missionary zeal and tries again to read from the Koran. He tells me that Jesus is not God but one of a line of Prophets. The most important to him of course is Mohammed. He is the latest and most important having spoken the most recent word of

God that must be transmitted to every person throughout the world. He tells me that Mohammed was a soldier by profession with very definite and strong beliefs. He taught that the sword should enforce the law of God if persuasion fails. So a true believer is obliged to spread the word at all cost and if he dies in the cause, everlasting paradise will be his reward. Non- believers or the infidel are expendable and so his and every good Muslims mission is to convert others until all the peoples of the world are believers in God and his Prophet. By now I had reached saturation point and started to nod off. The night passed with the occasional prayer and minor disturbance but I obtained enough sleep to support the next day's travels. In the morning I make for the road south and Abdullah walks with me through the town. At the outskirts he says farewell and returns to his mosque probably thinking he has won a convert, meanwhile I await a truck to take me back to Iraq.

An uneventful and boring journey with the only point of interest being the land of the marsh Arabs in this extensive swampland with wooden houses on stilts and roads built on pontoon-like bridges. The vehicles jerk and bob along most precariously, I find it difficult to believe that more vehicles do not end up in the water. It takes a day or so of travel to reach solid ground and eventually I reach the Kuwaiti border. Here I am kept waiting for hours as the border guard does not speak English and he is not happy with my visa. I have to wait until his senior officer comes from H.Q. Meanwhile we drink tea and amuse ourselves by throwing stones to see who can hit the cement barrel on the checkpoint pole. The desert checkpoints amuse me in that firstly you have to search to find them in the open desert. Then after having your passport stamped the border guard has to walk out and manually lift up the swinging arm for the vehicle to drive between the posts when it would be much easier to drive straight past the posts. When the officer does eventually arrive he is satisfied that my visa is in order and by way of amends for the delay takes me in his car into Kuwait City.

Chapter Ten

A Maiden in Distress

Kuwait is a small country, about the size of Wales. It only has one town and that is Kuwait City, which is a very modern city with no history whatsoever. Until twenty years ago it was simply desert, now modernistic and even outrageously designed buildings are being created everywhere with what seems like little regard for an overall plan. Walking through the streets of this newly developed city I gaze at the buildings with their strange shapes and bright colours. Suddenly I stop in disbelief; there at my feet there is a cast iron manhole cover set neatly in the paving slabs. Embossed on its surface are the words CRADLEY HEATH – ENGLAND. I am standing on a piece of England or almost. Did the Local Authority really have to go all the way to the English Midlands to find manhole covers? With their weight the freight costs must have far exceeded their purchase price, but then there is no shortage of money out here.

Kuwaiti citizens do very well in this oil rich state. All public services like education, health and even the telephone and post are free. They are even given trees and shrubs for their gardens. The only thing they appear to pay for is water. Their only industry is oil and that pays for everything else. Everywhere I go I am treated like a foreign dignitary with visits to the newspaper printing works and the oil storage plant. I am given large glossy photographs of their latest enterprises of which they are very proud. It certainly is a completely different world to where I have been living for the past six months. All the people are pristine in their appearance and manners, their clothes are immaculate, usually bright white headdresses and caramel coloured gowns, heavily adorned with gold jewellery and that is just the men. Instead of being the rich man in town, here I am definitely the poorest. At the moment there is a huge fire burning out of control at one of the oil plants. It has been burning for a couple of weeks and lights up half the sky at night. An American called Red Adair has been brought in at great expense to try and put it out but he hasn't succeeded as yet.

Sitting in a teahouse in town, I am contemplating my existence and the need to get a job to support my enhanced lifestyle. To date my only offer has been to proof read for the English newspaper, which is printed on a weekly basis. I have met the editor and seen a few back copies, which are full of spelling mistakes and errors, but the work is not really my thing. Everything else I can think of is either too technical for me or requires speaking Arabic. Perhaps I could do "Shoe shine" on the street, but that would lower the tone of the neighbourhood and draw unwanted attention to myself.

I am just about to finish my drink when a young blond woman in her twenties bursts through the door and asks if anyone speaks English. Everyone looks at her as she stands in the doorway wearing a sari! I am the only one who responds with a 'Yes'. She approaches me and breathlessly says she needs help quickly. I ask her to sit down and tell me her problem. She sits on the edge of the chair opposite and leans on the table speaking quietly into my face.

"I am English and I have escaped from a Prince's harem. I need a safe place to hide and a replacement passport so that I can get back to England".

"Well this is a novel chat up line, but just in case its true we had better make a move before the guards catch up with you. Walking the streets on your own in this dress will draw rapid attention and a swift arrest. In my company you might get a little further and hopefully as far as the British Embassy, lets go".

I know the embassy district but not the British Embassy in particular, so we walk briskly in the general direction. We try to avoid any concentration of people or police, taking a few erratic turns and doubling back once to avoid a gathering that may have been nothing to do with our situation but we cannot afford to risk a confrontation with so many. Eventually with great relief we find the British Embassy, the door is open and we walk up to the reception desk, which is manned by a young Kuwaiti man who looks somewhat surprised by our arrival. His English is poor and he goes for assistance returning with another Kuwaiti who speaks English a little better.

"No, the Ambassador is not here, please come tomorrow."

"We cannot do that, this is urgent, and we have nowhere safe to go".

We sit on a sofa in reception to consider our situation. Surely there must be someone we can explain to, but no. The one man returns from whence he came and the other sits at the desk looking bored and when we try to engage him he just repeats "Tomorrow".

After twenty minutes of stalemate, I suggest we try the American Embassy. This only occurs to me because I had witnessed how supportive they had been to Lee in other countries when he had sought assistance. We take directions and walk about a mile further along the road, right out of town. We enter a similar reception area and are confronted by a young Kuwaiti, who also says,

"No the Ambassador is not in."

Our hearts sink again. There must be an Ambassadors meeting on. It is almost dark now and we have nowhere to go. Search parties for this young lady will be well organised by now. While we sit considering our situation the man at the reception desk asks if it is important.

"Yes, yes it is very urgent".

He leaves the reception and returns a few minutes later with a smartly dressed middle aged lady.

"Hello, I am the Ambassadors wife, how can I help you?"

Liz, whose name I know by now, retells the story she had told me on our walk to the Embassy. How she had been held in a palace for the past three months until lunchtime today, when she escaped in a laundry basket amongst the soiled linen. Once in the city laundry she released herself and escaped through the streets until she came to the café where she met me. She tells how there are dozens of European and Scandinavian girls within the palace who have been lured there by one means or another. They are well provided for with all personal comforts and a wholesome diet. Liz and many of the other girls have never actually seen the prince. In Arabia princes and sheiks are in plentiful supply, there seems to be one to the square mile. Liz tells us the harem is rather like a girls club but with nothing to do. The only recent excitement was when three girls were selected to accompany the prince to his chateau in Switzerland. Liz who comes from London originally responded to an advert in the Sunday Times to work as a nanny. She was interviewed, accepted and flown out to Kuwait, before she realised she had been entrapped. The Ambassador's wife listened mouth agape.

"Incredible! Yes of course we will help. My husband will negotiate with the British Ambassador for a replacement passport, meanwhile you can both stay here until it is all sorted out".

The Ambassador's wife, Mrs B. seems a wonderful lady and takes us through to our rooms and fits Liz out with some more appropriate clothes. Then we return to the living quarters for tea, biscuits and a further chat before retiring to our rooms for a rest. We are later invited down for an evening meal with the family. The Ambassador is intrigued with Liz's story but says nothing can be done other than arrange for repatriation. He takes Liz's details and phones them through to the British Embassy who say they will start proceedings immediately and a new passport should be available in about three days. Liz and I retire to our rooms for a good night's sleep.

At breakfast the next morning Mrs B. who is obviously a good organiser with several staff to assist her with the running of the Embassy, calls a meeting and gives the staff their duties, including Liz and myself who seem now to be part of the household. I am to drive Mrs B. and Liz into town to buy Liz some new clothes and do some household shopping and then in the afternoon we are to take her two boys, aged seven and ten years, for a swim on the beach at the rear of the Embassy. It all seems to go to everyone's satisfaction and Mrs B. in particular appears well pleased with the day's events. After tea Liz and I take a walk back to the beach and sit watching the sunset, Liz is obviously emotionally upset; she became tearful and softly thanks me for my efforts in bringing her to safety. She can't believe how she has been seduced by the promise of a well paid job in a warm and affluent country. The reality of being kept with dozens of other girls in sumptuous luxury doesn't compensate for the loss of freedom and the absence of all the interests that young women in the 1960's had come to expect. Liz and I sat arms around each other, tears in her eyes she wonders whether her over cheerful letters home actually arrived. She is apprehensive about the response she will receive in England from her family and friends. I reassure her that she is now safe and soon to be back home with a great story to tell them all. We get on very well together and for the next few days we enjoy sharing duties and treats handed out by Mrs B. Then Liz's new passport suddenly arrives and things happen quickly. Mr B. takes her to the airport himself, after tears, kisses and embraces all round it feels like the end of an era.

Liz has gone I feel a void and an expectancy that the B's would think I should move on as well. Because we arrived together they tended to see us as a couple and I think the Ambassador really expected me to accompany Liz back to England. However, while he was at the airport I had a good chat with Mrs B. She confided in me that her husband is concerned about diplomatic repercussions not just with the Kuwaiti's but also with the British.

Firstly, regarding his involvement as an American and also what might be seen as possible negligence by the British authorities. There is also the question of the harem, does it exist or not? What the prince does in his own country is his business and cannot be questioned by the Americans or the British. However, if foreign nationals are being held against their will, can anything be done? Not unless they can escape and seek asylum like Liz did. Mrs B. then surprises me by saying she would like me to stay on for a while. She feels that I fit in well and that I am good for her boys. She would like me to give them lessons in English and for me to try and emphasise my English accent, which is apparently a sought after attribute in America at this time. Now at least I feel easier about staying on for a while and building myself up with good food and a relaxed lifestyle. After a few days of helping around the house running errands into the city and supervising the boys in English and swimming I am well integrated into the household.

Not quite a member of the family but almost and the servants are happy to do my bidding as long as it does not clash with Mrs B's orders. Towards the end of the week Mrs B. asks me if I will take on another duty. I wonder what is coming, as she is apprehensive in her manner and I cannot think what else I can possibly do. Then she drops what to me is a bombshell. Her husband is holding a diplomatic party on the Saturday evening. There are to be visiting dignitaries from America and friendly Ambassadors and their wives from Kuwait and the Trucial States. Ok, so I will keep clear of the entertainments room and make myself scarce.

"No, on the contrary we would like it very much if you would act as Master of Ceremonies and organise the evening, introduce the guests, ensure the servants keep the food and drink flowing, operate the sound system and the music".

Oh well, I cannot really say no when they are being so good to me but I will need help and advice on what to do and when.

"Yes of course" I reply.

I am assured the Ambassador will give me a guest list and demonstrate the sound system. Mrs B. will show me the routines for the food, drink and entertainment.

"What entertainment is that?" I ask hesitantly.

"Well, party games and charades, that always goes well. If you can do that it will enable my husband and myself to devote ourselves completely to our guests and so ensure the evening will be a greater success".

So they have obviously discussed it and decided between themselves. Though I am not one for the limelight, I am okay with props and lighting but if I have to speak in public I would rather not. However, Mrs B. is just as good a diplomat as her husband and I cannot find the words to decline. She assures me of her full support, including lessons in charades, which I never played even as a child. Mrs B. explains that since some of the guests have limited English mime works very well. They also have an extra category to the book, film or play, which is 'Famous Personality' from the local or world stage. She arranges a practice session for me with the staff to ensure I have the right idea.

Come the Saturday evening I am a bag of nerves. I am dressed in one of the Ambassador's suits complete with bow tie, pacing up and down in the reception area. As the guests arrive they pass their coats to one of the staff who then tell me who they are. I greet them and walk them to the open door of the entertainment room, stepping inside I then announce them to the assembly. I have a sheet of paper with their names, title and phonetics where necessary, which I have been familiarising myself with on and off throughout the afternoon. The American and European names are no problem but some of the Arabic ones are tricky and I have to sneak a look at the phonetics in the few paces between the reception and the entrance door. The Queen of Egypt puzzled me, Mrs B. explained that she was the former Queen but with the dissolution of the monarchy in Egypt she had taken sanctuary in Kuwait. However, I was not to mention 'former' as she was understandably a little touchy about it.

When all the guests had arrived and were mingling I had to turn down the music and announce the buffet was open. The servants then slid back a partition to reveal the buffet displayed at the far end. Now I need to ensure that the glasses are topped up and as soon as a buffet platter becomes less than half full it goes back to the kitchen for refill and rearrangement. I am asked to allow one and a half hours for chew and chat and then call order for the entertainment. I decide to let it go nearer two hours to make sure everyone becomes well acquainted and has sufficient drink to relax. Calling order I briefly explain the rules of charades for those who are unsure. I start the session off myself and I am spotted almost straight away as Lawrence of Arabia. The English, Americans and Germans are good at this and appear to hold the stage, the Arabs are not so quick and the poor old Queen of Egypt does not really know what is happening except when her glass needs topping up. Everything seems to be going very well until some bright spark sits on a dining chair, smiling and waving, then he loudly claps his hands twice and falls on the floor motionless. There was a deathly silence throughout the room, then Mr B. steps forward and says,

"Whether or not that was supposed to be JFK we will all stand and take a minutes silence in tribute."

Well that finishes the charades, so on comes the music and I am now disc jockey for the rest of the evening. About half of the company take to the floor for dancing. The business chat and socialising continues into the early hours. As people drift away the Ambassador and his wife see them all personally to the door and their awaiting cars. Finally, there remains just the staff and myself clearing up, Mr and Mrs B. come over to me with a Jack Daniels and a sincere thank you for my efforts. I go to bed exhausted and relieved that at least I didn't mess up. The next week Mr B. said the British Ambassador was enquiring if I was available to be Master of Ceremonies at his party in two weeks time.

"Err, no sorry I am engaged."

However I did do a couple more parties for the American Ambassador before I left.

Spring is in the air and the weather is definitely getting hotter. I receive a letter from Lee to say he is now in Pakistan but he has heard nothing from Rami and Mel and he feels they should have contacted him by now. I am now receiving regular letters from home and able to make phone calls courtesy of the Ambassador. My mother is asking me to return to England, at least for a while. My old work colleagues are keen for me to return and the Director personally contacted my mother to say he has a job waiting for me. I am torn between moving onto Pakistan to meet up with Lee or return home. Mrs B. is happy for me to stay on but her maternal instincts are that I should return to England for a while. Then I receive another letter from Lee to say he is waiting no longer but returning to the more moderate climate of Europe, so I decide to return to England via the land route of Iraq, Turkey and Germany. I may even meet up with Lee on the road. I talk it through with Mrs B. and then she suggests that I phone home to tell my excited mother my decision. The Ambassador also writes to my mother to say how much they have enjoyed my company and that I am welcome to revisit at any time. I pack my few possessions and say my grateful farewells. I see this as the culmination of my adventure although there are several weeks of hard travelling before I finally reach home. There is the difficult journey once more across the desert and through the snowy mountains of Kurdistan and Turkey. Travelling in trucks that break down and skid off the road. Riding on horse-drawn sledges and dodging hungry wolves still to be endured.

I realise my life will never be the same again. The near death experiences made a momentous impression forever etched in my mind. I will never again have the opportunity, health and strength to endure the hardships, excitement and character building escapades of that year.

Postscript

The reader may be interested to know what happened to some of those people I met since the completion of my adventure.

Madame Malet exchanged Christmas cards for several years until they ceased in the late 1960`s.

In 1967 Lee came to stay with me in England and we spent a week visiting the tourist sites of the Midlands and reminiscing about our adventures. He returned to California, married, had two children and we corresponded for several years.

Rami returned to Spain with Mel who stayed in Spain while he returned to New York for treatment. Unfortunately he died on route presumably from another hypoglycaemic attack. His belongings were returned to his mother in Hawaii, she found my address in his papers, and wrote asking me to give her some memories of our travels together, which I duly did.

In 1967 Mrs Mattar wrote me a very long letter telling me how her dear husband was shot dead in the Garden whilst going in peace to open the gate to the advancing Israeli army at the onset of the six day war. She and her daughter narrowly escaped death by hiding in the tomb. Today the Garden Tomb is one of the biggest Christian places of pilgrimage in Israel receiving over two hundred thousand visitors a year. It is a very different place today and a glimpse of it can be seen on the Garden Tomb website.

In Tehran today the Goldstan Palace is open to the public as the Government wishes the Iranian people to see the opulence in which the Shah and his family used to live.

Liz, the young lady who escaped from the harem in Kuwait returned to London and I was surprised to never hear from her again. Maybe her experience of Kuwait was something she didn't wish to be reminded of. The American Ambassador and his wife continued to exchange Christmas cards for many years, but I never did return to Kuwait

The many good people of the Middle East who helped me continuously on my travels and who by nature are in the main a caring and considerate people are now embroiled in horrific conflict that can be seen daily on the world news. This living hell I am ashamed to say has not been helped by the American and British involvement. I pray like millions of others, for an early end to the bloodshed and turmoil, though I am not optimistic of a settlement in the near future.

Acknowledgments

To my wife Sally for typing the manuscript.
My son Andrew and his wife Jo for their technical assistance.

Bibliography

"Eothen" by Alexander Kinglake
Published by J M Dent & Sons
The Gospels of the New Testament
The Mail on Sunday
Review on Iran 22-4-2007

Printed in the United Kingdom
by Lightning Source UK Ltd.
124216UK00003B/130-171/A

9 781434 330727